the FORTRESS by the RIVER

Receiving God's Heart in the Face of the **Impossible**

BOOK 2 OF THE **HEARTWORK SERIES**

the FORTRESS by the RIVER

Receiving God's Heart in the Face of the Impossible

MIKE AND KELSEY DOMENY

To the King of our hearts, Jesus Christ. You don't need us,
but choose to involve us in Your Kingdom-building work. May
You make much of Yourself through this book.

To you, overwhelmed and intimidated by the impossible.
God sees you and is eager to walk with you.

Contents

A Note from the Authors

While this book is presented as the second book of the Heartwork Series, we understand different readers will find themselves in different phases of God's work in their lives. If you feel like God has stacked the odds against you, and there are obstacles between where you are and where you want to be, this book is a great place to start.

Thank you for reading.

Chapter One

The Goal

It's got to be in the top ten Bible stories. Kids sing about it in Sunday school. If you've been in church for any length of time, you know the story in song. "Joshua fought the battle of Jericho, Jericho, Jericho. Joshua fought the battle of Jericho, and the walls came a-tumblin' down."

We love it! It's exciting! Preachers will tell us to "envision your Promised Land", and we just need to have faith in God to win our battles. Then the obstacles in our life will come a-tumblin' down!

You might think, "Man, if I could be more like Joshua—more bold, more faith-filled—then I could really get through this. If I had a mentor like Moses, and if I had Joshua's 'go-getter' attitude when he scouted the Promised Land, then my personal Jericho would be toast."

Maybe you are, in fact, a success-driven person. You eat goals for breakfast. For you, it's not a matter of *if* you'll reach the Promised Land, but *when*. And as much as it depends on you, you'll make sure "when" happens as soon as possible.

Or maybe you've been circling in the shadow of an impossible obstacle for some time now. A diagnosis. A financial burden. A relationship. For you, each day drains the hope that you'll ever live happily on the other side of it.

What is your "Jericho"? What is the obstacle that stands between you and where you want to be in life? What imposing barrier is impossible to ignore? If you could choose to see a victory over that obstacle either today or seven years from now, what would you pick? If you prefer to wait seven years, then you could probably stop here and return this book. But if you're a normal human struggling while you wait to see a victory over something that seems impossible, you're not alone, and this book is for you.

You see, there's a funny thing about the story of Joshua and Jericho. That battle is in the book of Joshua, chapter six. And do you know what comes before Joshua chapter six? Joshua chapters one, two, three, four, and five. Crazy, right? And even before the events of Joshua chapter one, we see Joshua make a few cameo appearances. Not to put too fine a point on it, but the story doesn't *end* with the Battle of Jericho, either. And in the grand scheme of the Bible, entering the Promised Land wasn't "happily ever after" for God's people. So there must be something more to this story than reaching the finish line of victory. There must be more than reaching a goal.

God doesn't have to give reasons for anything. He could simply tell us the way something is, and we should be able to accept it, no explanation necessary. So when God does give us an explanation, I find it particularly interesting, like in this verse:

Before Joshua would lead the conquest into the Promised Land, God already told Israel that the process would not be a quick one. "The Lord your God will drive those nations out ahead of you little by little. You will not clear them away all at once..." (Deuteronomy 7:22). And here's the reason: "otherwise the wild animals would multiply too quickly for you."

Can you picture that? God could have said the word, and every enemy stronghold in the Promised Land would have been flattened. Every idolatrous pagan would have been wiped out. Israel could have waltzed into their new real estate in peace and celebration, without a single conflict on the horizon. But God knew better than to fulfill His own promise all at once. They did not have the population, the systems, and the mindsets necessary to dwell in the land. There would be a gap between what they received and what they could control, and here's something God knows that we tend to ignore: *dangerous things grow in the gap*. It's one thing to own the land. It's another thing to possess it.

Could this be why your ministry, business, or job has not taken off? What if this is why your church attendance hasn't exploded? Maybe this is why God hasn't zapped you with a "perfect" marriage, family, and workplace. What if these things actually happened? Can you honestly say you have the character, capacity, wisdom, and experience to keep them from crashing down again?

A father's shoe immediately falls off his infant son's feet. An immature heir blows through a million-dollar inheritance. In the same way, a goal achieved too quickly will be lost just as quickly. God's pace—undoubtedly slower than you would prefer—gives time and space for you to *receive God's heart and grow into the kind of person He wants you to be at the finish line.*

The danger is, if you don't seek God's pace, He may allow you to try to push forward at your own pace. A particularly driven person can set goals, break them into yearly, quarterly, and weekly to-do lists, and crush today's tasks before brunch. Such a pace runs the risk of achieving a destination your character has not had the time to grow into. Too many child celebrities, megastar pastors, and young entrepreneurs serve as sobering examples of the downfall that occurs when opportunities outpace character. The risk for Christians isn't diminished; it's increased. Don't think just because your work is "kingdom work," that God gives you free rein to go about it in your own time and way. *God is less invested in your to-do list, and completely invested in your "to-be" list.* Who you are, and who you are becoming, are of particular interest to God. The work is secondary.

Consider how Ian Simkins puts it, "You are an image bearer with work to do. Not a work-doer with an image to maintain."

The process

For years, Kelsey and I (Mike) wanted to write this book. Correction: For years, we wanted to *have written* this book. That's quite a different thing. We wanted to be the authors who had this book on the shelf, who gave it to friends, and who could stand on a stage to share the stories and lessons inside. We didn't *really* want to be the authors who spent solid hours with our heads back in our chairs, gazing through the ceiling, until we could put twelve coherent words together before deleting them again. Beyond that, we know what happens to Christian authors; God forces them to live out the message of their book. And we *certainly* didn't want that—again! We learned that lesson the hard way when the launch date of my first book, *Thrown off Script*, was overshadowed by an appointment at the unemployment office three months into the 2020 pandemic. That wasn't in our script, that's for sure. And now? We shuddered to think what God would do as we wrote a book about God's pace through obstacles.

Ultimately, we wanted to reach the *goal* of writing a book; we didn't want to go through the *process* of writing a book. We wanted to have finished a to-do list. We didn't want to consider that God was working on a "to-be" list. And sure enough, the years-long process of writing this book has exposed us to a crucible of character-refining circumstances: financial drought, church hurt, lost friends, closed doors, aimlessness, and confusion.

While this book doesn't address those specific challenges at length, it is saturated with the lessons we learned from "the process," mirrored in the story of Joshua and Israel. We have learned how to be (not fully, but willingly) humble, present, trusting, content, patient, counter-cultural, faithful, hopeful, and vulnerable. That "to-be" list will keep us busy for the rest of our lives!

So what about you? God cares more about what kind of person you are when you cross the finish line, than *when* you cross it. So much so, in fact, that the process may take so long that you think God has forgotten about the goal altogether.

But *for God, the growth is the goal.* Mark that down. Let that sink in. Kelsey and I will bring it back to the surface throughout this book, because it bears repeating and it's easy to forget the purpose behind our pain.

Pastor Chuck Swindoll observed, "When I ask people when they really grew spiritually, they never describe an easy time. Never."[1] God's goal is to develop the fruit that only grows during the process of approaching and circling the imposing fortress on the other side of a raging river, and that takes time. The growth is the goal.

THE GROWTH IS THE GOAL.

When you read the Bible and watch God interact with His people, you shouldn't be surprised. The prequel to this book, *The Mountain in the Desert*, watched God lead the Israelites "the long way" and stop frequently to teach them about Himself. While the story of Israel in the wilderness, led by Moses, was about the process of learning who

God was, the story of Israel entering the Promised Land, led by Joshua, is about the process of learning who God wants them to be.

You'll find *pace* to be another frequent concept in this book. Sometimes God moves faster and more immediately than is comfortable to you. Often He moves slower. As you go through the process of studying this story and applying it to your own journey, Kelsey and I pray that you, too, learn to embrace God's pace and grow into who God wants you to be.

One thing is clear from the story of Joshua: Joshua began to embrace God's pace long before he was tapped to lead a single conquest. One of Joshua's cameos from Moses' story demonstrates a crucial mindset we can have when it comes to our role in becoming who God wants us to be.

Stay late

As Moses continued to lead God's people out of Egypt, they weren't exactly following *Moses* himself. Their routine was that they followed a pillar of cloud during the day, and at night, they followed a pillar of fire. These pillars were God's presence among them. If God moved, they moved. If God stopped, they stopped and set up all their tents and made camp.

> It was Moses' practice to take the Tent of Meeting and set it up some distance from the camp. Everyone who wanted to make a request of the Lord would go to the Tent of Meeting outside the camp. Whenever Moses went out to the Tent of Meeting, all the people would get up and stand in the entrances of their own tents. They would all watch Moses until he disap-

peared inside. As he went into the tent, the pillar of cloud would come down and hover at its entrance while the Lord spoke with Moses. When the people saw the cloud standing at the entrance of the tent, they would stand and bow down in front of their own tents.

Inside the Tent of Meeting, the Lord would speak to Moses face to face, as one speaks to a friend. Afterward Moses would return to the camp, *but the young man who assisted him, Joshua son of Nun, would remain behind in the Tent of Meeting* (Exodus 33:7-11, emphasis mine).

Kelsey has a couple of good friends she loves talking to. We call them "soul-feeders," but now that I write it out, that description seems creepy. Soul-*fillers*, maybe? Anyway, whenever she says she's going to meet up with them to chat, I know to not expect her to come home anytime soon. If it's lunch, expect it to be dinner, too. If it's in the evening, expect them to pop popcorn and talk on the couch until 2:00am.

After a long day of talking with God, "as one speaks to a friend", like it says (isn't it amazing that God, who split the sea, and who appeared as a pillar of fire by night, allows us to speak to him *at all*, let alone like a friend?), Moses would say,

"Alright, Joshua, I'm off to bed. Well done today," and Joshua would say,

"Thank you, sir. Good night. If it's alright with you, though, I'd like to stay a bit later."

"That's fine, see you in the morning."

And then Joshua would stay and talk with God by lamplight, one on one, late into the night.

Joshua stayed when everyone else went home. That's the character that gets God's attention. That's the kind of relationship with God that says, "I'm willing to go at God's pace." When God says, "be strong and courageous because I am with you," it's a whole lot easier to believe it when you've chosen to be with Him.

Do you, like Joshua in the tent of meeting, have a regular time and place to talk to him? Maybe first thing in the morning, or on the drive to and from work, or the last thing before bed.

That's good and valuable, but let's think a step further. When was the last time you stayed *late* to talk to God? Maybe you could sit in the parking lot for a few extra minutes. Stay up a little longer after everyone else has gone to sleep. Make the church custodian have to kick you out because the service ended a couple of hours ago.

I have to admit, too often, I try to make my time with God quick so I can start the next thing, or go to sleep. As a Christian, I'll say I'm looking forward to "spending eternity with God", but if I'm honest, I find myself getting distracted before I've spent even a solid hour with Him here on earth.

We're taught to pray the Lord's prayer, "your Kingdom come on earth as it is in heaven." Maybe we can bring His Kingdom to earth even a little bit by spending more time with Him here. Jesus says in John 15:4, "Remain in me, and I will remain in you." Only by remaining in the soil can a seed begin to sprout and grow and bear fruit.

So today, I encourage you to stay later. Abide. Carve out some extra time to remain. Maybe you sense God telling you, "Hey, we haven't hung out much lately. Let's talk for a bit." Or maybe you feel like God is preparing you to step up in responsibility. At work, at church, in your family. Set your pace with God by spending more time with Him. Ask Him who He wants you to be, and humbly express your willingness to be changed.

I'm honored you're reading this book, and I'm sure you have other things to do after this chapter. But maybe put this away for a little bit, and before you start the next thing, talk with God like you'd talk to a friend. Stay behind a while, just you and God, and practice embracing God's pace.

Joshua's most important battles weren't against Canaanites and fortified cities. Joshua's most important battles were against the natural desire to rush God's timing. He didn't achieve victories by hustling. He achieved victories by abiding.

Chapter Two

The Foreigner

Back in Joshua's day, the Promised Land (or Canaan, as it was known to anyone other than the Israelites) was not its own nation. The region contained many individual cities, each of which functioned like its own little kingdom, complete with a king and small army. Jericho was perhaps the most impressive city in Canaan. Its imposing shadow fell on busy trade routes, and was strategically embedded between a wide river and jagged mountains. The city itself was well-fortified. Theoretically, if an army could somehow conquer Jericho, it would send a definitive message to the other cities in the region that there's a new boss in town.

God set His sights on Jericho, and made it the primary target of the conquest of Canaan. Joshua wanted to know a bit more about what lay ahead of them, so he sent two spies ahead to scout out the city.

The two men donned their sunglasses and fanny packs, and settled into the role of innocent tourists. "Oh wow! Jericho! The City of Palms! I can't believe we finally made it! I hear they have the best figs!"

As they entered the gate, they marveled at the outer wall.

"Wow... how high would you say that is? Thirty? Forty feet? Boy oh boy, I sure do feel safe here! And look!" Their eyes widened, "Another wall!"

The spies tried to hide their disheartened faces as they gawked at a second, inner wall, itself a couple stories high. They received suspicious side-eyes as they ran their hands along the inner face of the mudbrick fortification, occasionally giving it a solid smack.

"Yep! Solid construction! I bet this bad boy could keep out Pharaoh himself, huh?! No way this thing is ever coming down!"

They laughed nervously, a little too loudly. "Hahah, yeah! Jericho's the best! I hope it's here forever!"

They extended their selfie sticks. Their camera scraped the ground in an attempt to capture the striking height of the walls behind them.

They got the attention of a woman, slinkily draped against her doorframe. "Hey strangers... looks like you could use a new friend..." The setting sun had already disappeared behind the wall, casting a dark shadow over the woman and her dimly-lit establishment.

"Wow, the folks here in Jericho are so welcoming! Actually, ma'am, we were hoping to get a picture of us with this wall! Would you mind taking one for us?"

With a disgruntled raise of an eyebrow, the woman blew a strand of hair out of her eyes and took the camera from the men. "Alright, boys, say 'Yahweh!'"

"Yah—wait—what?"

Before the men could catch the camera tossed hastily back at them, the woman grabbed their wrists indelicately and shoved them through her door. "Today's special: two for the price of one!" she half-shouted back out to the street in case anyone was paying attention. She slammed the door behind her.

"Good gracious, ma'am, I think you've got the wrong impression…" one of the spies attempted to de-escalate while keeping his cover.

"Quiet! Get to the roof." The mysterious woman's hurried, no-nonsense demeanor stood in stark contrast to their first impression as she shoved them up the back stairs.

"What do you want from us?"

"Discretion, for starters." The woman lowered her voice and maintained a frightening intensity. "I know who you are. And judging by some of the looks you were shot by the wall, I don't think I'm the only one."

She unfurled a pair of unassuming gray blankets over several bundles of flax that had been left to dry on the flat roof. As she peered over the edge, she inhaled sharply at the sight of four armed men at her door, below. Their knocks resonated throughout the house.

"Open up. By order of the king!"

"Under there. Now." The woman flicked her painted nails toward the blankets as she turned toward the stairs, barely taking time to glance back at the two men. "Stay here until I come back," she hissed and hurried down to the door, which was being beaten a bit more aggressively this time. Taking only a couple seconds to adjust her hair and bodice, she opened the door and clipped her hand to her hip confidently.

"Lucky me. Not every day you boys from the citadel come to visit. Except you, Hargin. You forgot your belt last time." She winked at the guard on the left.

The other guards briefly broke their focus to raise a mocking eyebrow at the now red-faced guard. The leader shook his head to regain control of the conversation. "Shut up, harlot. Where are the two men who were here earlier? They're spies. Enemies of the king." He shoved past the woman gruffly to survey the room.

"Two men...? Honey, if I could count every man that came through this door, I'd be running the treasury. Can't help you." She turned and started back toward an inner room.

The guard grabbed her shoulder, but she whipped around sharply before he could force her turn.

"Most guys have to pay good money to grab me like that." Her tone was much more threatening than flirtatious. "Lucky for you, I like you." Her dry sarcasm was not lost on the man.

"No games, harlot. Two men. Accents that are unknown to your ear. They smell of the desert. I know they're here."

"Oh!" a look of recognition flashed across her face. "Those two." The guards leaned in, finally onto a lead. "I never caught their names. I called them Barley and Flax. Looked just like skinny bundles with belts around their waist. Anyway. Yes, they were here. But they just wanted to talk. I don't have time for that, so I kicked them out. That goes for you, too."

She crossed her arms and nodded toward the door. "Both of them skipped out the gates at dusk just before they closed. I don't know where they went, but you can probably catch up with them if you hurry."

The main guard was unsatisfied with the interrogation overall, but it was the only information they had. He nodded at his men, who hurriedly began their pursuit. "If you lie to me, harlot," he leaned forward intimidatingly, "I would hate to see what would happen to that pretty little face of yours..."

"Aw, you think I'm pretty?" she batted her eyelashes.

With a disgruntled huff and a slam of the door behind him, the guard was gone. The woman exhaled slowly. Her eyes darted over toward the stairs to the rooftop, and, after glancing once more out the window, she returned to the two men.

She flung the blankets away unceremoniously, revealing the huddled men now struck by the gravity of the situation. They had heard everything.

"How…" one man picked a strand of flax from his hair as he struggled to process what happened. "How did we get discovered so quickly? You… the guards…"

The other man jabbed him in the ribs. "What he means to say is thank you. My name is Sal. This is Makir. We are in your debt. And you are…?"

"In big trouble with the king if he finds you here," she quipped as she bustled around the dark rooftop to assemble some provisions.

"No, really. Your name?"

"My name…?" she softened and paused. "Rahab." Her name fell off her lips as if she hadn't been asked to utter it in quite some time.

"The God of Abraham, Isaac, and Jacob bless you, Rahab."

"I hope so…" her voice drifted off ever so briefly before getting back to business. "To answer your question, it was your accent. Doesn't sound like the travelers we're used to. Sounds like if an Edomite had a cousin who spent too much time in Egypt."

Sal raised a thoughtful eyebrow and nodded to concede. Makir pressed the point. "But why are we so quickly considered enemies of Jericho?"

Rahab's eyes widened. "It's not just Jericho. This entire land is terrified of your Yahweh. Word has spread like the locusts that devoured Egypt. How your God made a path through the Red Sea. Swallowed up Pharaoh's army. Sihon. Og. If your God could wipe out the kings on the other side of the river, there's no river wide enough, and no wall high enough to stop Him! Look around! Every heart in this city has melted in fear. No one dares stand up and fight against your God!"

Rahab suddenly became aware of how her increasingly excited voice might carry into the street. She hushed herself. "I'm convinced. Yahweh your God is the one true God over the entire earth, and I know He has given you this land and this city."

The men sat in silent shock. This woman remembered their history of Yahweh's victories more than some of their own people. And, to their shame, she had more faith that Yahweh could win this battle than they did.

"Well..." Sal finally spoke softly, measured. "We owe you our life. What can we do for you?"

"Swear to me," Rahab reached out and clenched the hand of each man with hers. "Swear to me by Yahweh that you will show mercy to me and my family." Rahab quieted her voice to the most brittle whisper, "When this city falls under Yahweh—and I know it will fall—promise me you'll let me live. Me and my family members." She gripped the men's hands even tighter, "Please. Family means every-thing to me."

"On our lives, we will repay your mercy with mercy." Makir nodded in agreement as Sal spoke solemnly. "If you keep our secret, we'll keep our word."

"Yes!" Rahab squealed, and released their hands. She, without thinking, kissed Sal on the cheek as she stood up to grab the supply pouches she had hastily assembled. Sal blushed, still stunned. Rahab's pace quickened. "Now come with me, you need to leave the city."

Rahab ran down the stairs, Sal and Makir in tow, and led them not out the front door, but down a back hallway into an inner room. She flung apart luxurious red curtains to reveal a north-facing window that looked out over the countryside.

"If you go right, along the road, you'll be spotted. Go left. Hide in the hills. Wait three days, and the king will stop hunting you." Rahab coiled a length of cord that had been used to gather the heavy curtains. She tied one end to a bedpost, and tossed the other end out the window. She leaned out and looked down. The end of the rope dangled a few feet off the ground. With an approving shrug, she made eye contact once again with the men.

"Before you go. One last thing. You know how the Death Angel killed the firstborn of every Egyptian, but the Hebrew homes had blood on the doors and were spared?"

Sal and Makir nodded slowly, unaware of how open their mouths were. Yes, they knew. How did she know? Word really did spread.

"What can I do to be saved? Do I need blood on my door, too? "Uh…" Sal and Makir looked at each other, at a bit of a loss for words and ideas. "This!" Makir noted the red rope hanging out the window. "Once we're gone tonight, you should gather it back up so the guards don't suspect anything. But then, when our people approach the city, hang this from the window again."

Sal nodded and carried the idea, "This will be the signal between us. But only this house will be spared. Anyone you want to be safe must be in this house. If they even step foot into the street, we can't guarantee their safety. But just as this house saved our lives, it will save the life of anybody inside on that day. Agreed?" Sal extended his hand.

"Agreed." Rahab gave his hand a firm shake, and hurried the men out the window. They did as she suggested, and after three days, they returned to Joshua on the other side of the river.

"Sal! Makir!" Joshua breathed a sigh of relief. "What took you so long? I was beginning to think we lost you!"

The men's eyes were glowing with anticipation. "The Lord has given us this land. Everyone's already terrified of us!"

"Praise Yahweh! But... what's that on your cheek?" He suspiciously eyed a red lip-shaped stain on Sal's cheek.

Sal put his hand to his face, mortified as Makir laughed, "Let's just say it's a promise to a friend."

This story of Rahab feels like a brief departure from the story of Joshua. That's because, frankly, it is. During this time, Joshua and the rest of Israel (except for two spies) are, what, camping? Waiting? Some eager Israelites I'm sure wondered what they were waiting for.

But unbeknownst to Joshua and the Israelites, God was also waiting. And it had nothing to do with Joshua or His nation. God was waiting for the sweet smell of faith to waft up from a doomed heathen fortress.

It's fascinating, isn't it? Here we have Rahab, a prostitute in a pagan city. She hears, through the rumors that spread from the locals living between Jericho and Egypt, that this Israelite nation is winning impossible victories because of their God. And now they're here, on her doorstep, and she puts all these pieces together very quickly. She knows their God is all-powerful. And her people don't stand a chance against Him.

Hold up a minute! It wasn't that long ago that *God's own people* were whining, "The people in the land are too strong for us!" "I wanna go back to Egypt!" "We're gonna die!" And they're the ones who walked through the Red Sea. They're the ones who picked up manna from heaven. How in the world does this *pagan prostitute*, who hasn't actually seen any of this, have more faith in what God can do than the chosen people who have walked with God all this time?

Like really! We need to answer this! Because I know people—shoot, I *am* people—who have been walking with God for years, and are still like, "Life is too hard! I wanna go back to the way things used to be! We're not gonna make it through this!" For real, what are we missing?

But then Rahab doesn't just *talk* about faith. She *acts* on it. She recognizes her people don't stand a chance against God, so she decides she won't stand against Him. She'll surrender to God and ask for mercy. This pagan prostitute knows she's headed for destruction, she knows her only chance is to surrender, and hopes that this God is as merciful as He is powerful.

Whether you've been walking with God, or standing opposed to God all this time, this woman is putting us all to shame right now with this radical faith. Actually, I take back the word "radical". It's just faith we all should have.

In fact, it's been memorialized in the Bible, in the book of Hebrews. Hebrews chapter 11 is sometimes called "The Hall of Faith", and it highlights some amazing acts of faith throughout history. Abraham, Isaac, Jacob, Joseph, Moses. We're talking major players here! If you've got a Fantasy Faith Draft, you want these guys on your team! And it goes on, verse 31...

"It was by faith that Rahab the prostitute was not destroyed with the people in her city who refused to obey God. For she had given a friendly welcome to the spies" (Hebrews 11:31).

Cycle-breaking faith

If you look around your family, your friends, your neighborhood or city, and you think, "I don't want to end up like that! They're headed for destruction. I can't control them, but I can control what I choose to do, and I choose to follow God even when it doesn't make sense, even if nobody else is with me," you're a cycle-breaker.

But here's what we hope you recognize about God from this story: God might be moving slow, and it has *nothing to do with you*. God has no problem making you wait if it means someone else has a chance to act in faith and break the cycle of death and destruction in their life.

GOD'S SLOWNESS MAY HAVE NOTHING TO DO WITH YOU.

Israel's wait meant Rahab's salvation. But that's not all. The best was still ahead for Rahab. Her name comes up again in the gospel of Matthew. Matthew's gospel opens with a genealogy, which sounds like a boring way to start a biography, but Matthew wrote to convince Jews that Jesus really was the Messiah, who came from the kingly line of David. Right in the middle of this genealogy, from Abraham to Jesus, we read this...

> Salmon was the father of Boaz (whose mother was Rahab).
> Boaz was the father of Obed (whose mother was Ruth).
> Obed was the father of Jesse.
> Jesse was the father of King David."
> ... [all the way down to Joseph, the husband of Mary]
> "Mary gave birth to Jesus, who is called the Messiah.
> (Matthew 1:5-6, 16)

Notice, not "Rahab the prostitute." Not "Rahab the harlot." Just... Rahab. A wife, a mother. The great-great-grandmother of King David. An ancestor of Jesus Christ himself.

God will exercise extreme patience when it comes to adding to His family. Sometimes, His patience affects you. So, while you're struggling in the painful slowness of waiting for God to move, understand He is moving, but it may not be about you. He could be slowing you down to let someone else catch up. There could be another character on a rabbit trail in your story who is a part of the future God is writing. His pace is allowing them the time they need to be part of it.

Redefining slow

Slow? No, God's not slow. You're thinking like a person bound by time.

"You must not forget this one thing, dear friends: A day is like a thousand years to the Lord, and a thousand years is like a day. The Lord isn't really being slow about his promise, as some people think. No, he is being patient for your sake. He does not want anyone to be destroyed, but wants everyone to repent" (2 Peter 3:8-9).

What looks slow to us is actually God's kindness and patience. When we feel like God is being slow about delivering on a promise, you can rest assured that He is being patient. That patience is what is allowing more and more people to come to know Him by the minute. Every minute God's final judgement is delayed is another minute for another person to repent. And every moment that He waits to bring to fruition all your heart desires might be moments that are allowing someone else the time to become grafted into the family tree.

Chapter Three

The Preparation

The spies brought back a good report from Jericho, the first target of Project Promised Land. The citizens were terrified of Israel and their God.

Israel must have been itching to charge ahead. The wait is finally over! It's the perfect time to strike, right?! Praise God! He made it so we can just waltz right into the Promised Land! Let's go! Let's do this!

"Early the next morning Joshua and all the Israelites left Acacia Grove and arrived at the banks of the Jordan River, where they camped before crossing" (Joshua 3:1).

Isn't that nice? Camping by the Jordan River. Resting up before the big conquest... Have you ever camped by a river? The soothing sounds of the water bubbling by. Relaxing, right? Puts you to sleep.

Well, I'm sure that'd be nice, but verse 15, which we'll talk about more in the next chapter, says the Jordan River was at flood stage. So Israel was *actually* camping uneasily adjacent to loud, intimidating, raging rapids.

They camped here for three days. The Promised Land lay tantalizingly close on the other bank. But they're camped on *this* side, with this scary, impossible obstacle in the way! Why? I think God wanted to give them a chance to watch and think and talk. Or maybe shout, because the river was so loud.

I bet some people wanted to muscle their way through. "We can't afford to wait any longer! We need to move in now while there's momentum!"

Some thought they should wait until the timing makes sense. "Let's just wait a few weeks for it to die down."

Some doubted. "How are we all gonna get across that?"

Some blamed God. "God's timing must be off."

Maybe one or more of those sound familiar.

This is all finish-line-thinking. Remember, God is less interested in when you cross the finish line, and more interested in the process of getting there. The growth is the goal. Waiting on the bank of the flooded river—waiting on the edge of what you see as impossible—is part of the growth process. How you spend this time matters more than crossing it.

How you wait matters. Wait well.

Waiting well

Other authors might start with a sports metaphor here. We don't have many of those, but we do have a Star Wars metaphor. Fellow nerds, this one's for you.

In Star Wars episode one (which we have to admit, is the least bad of the pre-trilogy), Qui Gon is in a climactic lightsaber duel with Darth Maul (if you don't know Star Wars, and you're still reading this, I bet you can still determine which one is the bad guy).

They're battling in a narrow corridor of a starship. In the middle of the duel, a series of force fields come up throughout the corridor, one of which separates Qui Gon from his enemy. The battle has to stop;

there's nothing they can do but wait. Qui Gon's apprentice, Obi Wan, had fallen behind. He's behind another force field further back, and he's frustrated he can't advance. But Qui Gon turns off his lightsaber, and kneels. Darth Maul is facing Qui Gon through a force field, and he's pacing like a caged tiger. But Qui Gon closes his eyes and kneels as he waits.

When there's nothing to do but wait, how do you wait?

You either spend this time worrying and doubting, pacing and plotting, or you spend it trusting and praying. *You either weaken your faith or strengthen your faith as you wait. It's one or the other.*

YOU EITHER WEAKEN YOUR FAITH OR STRENGTHEN YOUR FAITH AS YOU WAIT.

The waters look rough. You don't see a way forward. You're waiting. So wait well. Get your heart ready to be made stronger by going wherever Jesus leads you.

This is gonna be good.

Joshua told the people, "Consecrate yourselves, for tomorrow the Lord will do amazing things among you" (Joshua 3:5, NIV).

Can you feel the anticipation oozing from this verse? Oh boy, this is gonna be good. I don't know how comfortable you are interacting with your book, but if we were in the room together, I'd ask you to rub your hands together and say, "Get ready."

Consecrate is not a word we see outside the Bible that much. And you might wonder, "What does 'consecrate yourselves' mean?" Good question. Rub your hands together again and say, "Get ready." There you go. You answered your own question (even if you didn't just do that, I'll pretend you did).

When you get ready to eat, or get ready to meet someone after doing some dirty work, you wash your hands. In the same way, consecration means getting clean and getting ready. The Israelites would have to wash their hands, clothes, and bodies, and separate from anything that could make them physically or spiritually unclean before a special encounter with God.

In *The Mountain in the Desert*, we went into more detail about consecration as it was introduced in Exodus 19. Consecration requires an intentional stop to align our heart with God's, and that book contains an entire chapter that highlights different areas that may require our attention. And now, I'd like to continue that conversation in light of the process God uses to grow our hearts to become more like His.

Why does it matter?

While we modern Christians don't have to follow the same regulations around consecration as the Israelites did, the attitude and the spirit behind it is still true of us.

Paul instructs us in one of his letters, "Because we have these promises, dear friends, let us cleanse ourselves from everything that can defile our body or spirit. And let us work toward complete holiness because we fear God" (2 Corinthians 7:1).

That "cleansing" is a call to consecration today. And it should be our response to "these promises." What promises is Paul talking about? Great question. Every verse has a context, and every context has a context. Let's go back a few verses to see what he's talking about.

> As God said: 'I will live in them and walk among
> them. I will be their God, and they will be my people'.
> Therefore, come out from among unbelievers, and

separate yourselves from them, says the Lord. Don't touch their filthy things, and I will welcome you. And I will be your Father, and you will be my sons and daughters, says the Lord Almighty. (2 Corinthians 6:16-18)

There are a number of phrases in this passage that can get us tripped up and upset. This passage is not saying, "Don't hang out with unbelievers." It's not saying, "Unbelievers are dirty and you should keep your distance." Go read how Jesus interacted with unbelievers and you'll see that's not what it means.

What it is saying is God wants to live in us. He wants to walk with us. He wants everyone to know that we are His people, and He is our God. He wants others to know He is our Father, and we're His children. Those are promises rooted in the heart of God, which brings us back to the verse we started with: "Because we have these promises, dear friends, let us cleanse ourselves from everything that can defile our body or spirit. And let us work toward complete holiness because we fear God" (2 Corinthians 7:1).

The goal is complete holiness. That's the finish line. Why? Like Paul said, because we fear God. Not fear like being afraid. Fear like I would be horrified if someone looked at me right now and distanced themselves from God instead of getting closer to Him because of the way I'm living. I'd be horrified if someone got the wrong impression of God by looking at me.

And know this: they will be looking. Whether you enter a season of prosperity or a season of pain, there will be eyes on you. "Why do they have peace? Why do they seem so confident in their purpose? What makes them different?" Because God wants all those questions to point back to Him, He cares very much about you looking like Jesus now. They need to know that following Jesus makes a difference. Live differently so others can see following Jesus makes a difference.

Footholds

You have a real enemy who is determined to make you look as little like Jesus as possible, and drag you and others far away from God in the process.

Satan's most powerful tool is one you give him yourself: a foothold. One unrepented sin. One compromise. One unresolved outburst of anger. One person you're not willing to forgive. That's all Satan needs to walk right back into your life, no matter how much other righteous stuff you do.

Satan is perfectly fine if you dedicate some of your life to Jesus, or if you give up most of your sins and habits, because he's willing to play the long game. Peter explains,

When people escape from the wickedness of the world by knowing our Lord and Savior Jesus Christ and then get tangled up and enslaved by sin again, they are worse off than before. It would be better if they had never known the way to righteousness than to know it and then reject the command they were given to live a holy life. They prove the truth of this proverb: "A dog returns to its vomit." And another says, "A washed pig returns to the mud" (2 Peter 2:20-22).

To be frank, and a bit gross, consecration requires you to clean up the vomit. Wash away the mud. You may think, "I could never go back, after what God has saved me from!" Great! Make sure it's not an option. Clean up the foothold. Eliminate anything that connects you to your past sin so there is no bridge, no tunnel, no door, no way back to it.

Consecration isn't consecration if you keep your pet sins, your secret stashes, and your unequal partnerships. Remember, God is more interested in the process of getting to the finish line. The growth is the goal. The process is the promise. And in this chapter, we've seen that part of the process is to "get ready". Wait well. Clean up. Like Joshua told the people, get ready for God to do something amazing tomorrow.

You may be on the other shore of a victory in your own life, and while you may have one hand clinging to Jesus, your other hand is hanging on to something or someone that isn't interested in going where Jesus leads. God is saying "consecrate yourself." Separate from that. Let that go. Not because God is mean, but because *a victory in your life means nothing to God if you achieve it by looking like the world.* It's about God's glory, not your story. Glory, meaning God's reputation, credit, and fame. It means if we are supposed to be a reflection of God in this world, we need to take some Windex to our lives and address the dust and smudges that make it difficult to reflect God.

Your slow season right now may be because God is waiting on your consecration. He is waiting on your faithfulness to Him in one area or another. You left the vomit, but you know—and He knows—it's still there and you kinda think about it occasionally. You haven't fully separated from it. Or you're going to it every night in secret. Or you're accepting that someone in your house is going to it every day and you haven't cleaned it up to eliminate the source of the sin. Your consecration is crucial to moving forward. God will slow His pace to a halt if needed for you to get your house in order before Him. The destination across the river does not matter if you carry your sin across with you.

We need to get ourselves in position for God to do amazing things for us, but instead we spend so much time trying to get ourselves in position to do amazing things for God. We think about what we can *do* for Him. When He's calling us to slow down, consecrate, *be* who He is calling us to *be*, then He'll do amazing things among us.

To match God's pace right now, ask Him what you need to clean up in your life. Ask Him what is not holy in your life, in your mind, and in your heart that needs some bleach. And then do it. Get clean. Repent. Forgive. Reconcile. Reprioritize your time. Throw away the paraphernalia, cut off some relationships. Pray. Take care not to run ahead without slowing down for this imperative process of consecration.

Wait well. Get clean. Get ready. God's going to do something amazing among you tomorrow. We don't necessarily mean the next day on the calendar. We don't know when. But that's all the more reason to be ready when He shows up.

Chapter Four

The Risk

In the morning Joshua said to the priests, "Lift up the Ark of the Covenant and lead the people across the river." And so they started out and went ahead of the people (Joshua 3:6).

It wasn't easy being a priest in Israel.

When the tribe of Levi left Egypt with everyone else, they were excited to someday arrive in the Promised Land and hopefully settle down in villages and farms with their families. But at Mount Sinai, God chose the Levites to have a special role in His nation. They would be in charge of taking care of all the holy elements of the tabernacle (like a portable temple), and managing the details of sacrifices and interactions in the temple.

Consequently, they would not have land to call their own in the Promised Land. They would have to live in certain towns scattered throughout Israel, where they would help the rest of the nation interact with the holiness of God and get right with Him.

Their greatest honor was also their most intimidating responsibility. They were in charge of carrying the Ark of the Covenant. The Ark was effectively God's throne, and the most holy physical representation of God's presence with them. God gave specific instructions on how it was to be carried and treated, and only these priests could do this.

Now, put yourself in the shoes of these Levite priests. Not only because it will help us make a point in this chapter, but because that's what the Bible says to do!

"You are a chosen people. You are royal priests, a holy nation, God's very own possession..." (1 Peter 2:9).

Look at every single word God says about you:

Chosen - You are known and chosen by God.

People - You are placed in community if you belong to Christ.

Royal - You are a son or daughter of the King.

Priests- You help people approach God and get right with Him.

Holy - You are set apart for a special purpose.

Nation - You are a citizen of God's Kingdom.

God's very own possession - You are held and protected by a God who loves you and wants to show you off through His work in your life.

How do those words feel to try on? Comforting, empowering, maybe intimidating and above your pay grade? If you're feeling unworthy, these words feel misplaced or mistaken.

Just like God chose the Levites to carry His presence into the Promised Land, and to spend their lives helping others get right with God, God chose you to be like a priest and do the same. Why? Peter goes on to explain,

"...As a result, you can show others the goodness of God, for he called you out of the darkness into his wonderful light" (1 Peter 2:9).

Remember, this isn't God talking to Israel while they left Egypt on the way to the Promised Land. This is Peter talking to God's people in the New Covenant. As a child of God, your slavery to sin is behind you. The Promised Land is ahead of you. The light of Jesus is in you.

Entering the Promised Land isn't about fulfilling your dreams, living in prosperity, and finding comfort. It's about carrying the presence of God with you.

And to get there, Jesus says, "follow me." He doesn't say "Here's the address. Find your way and I'll see you there." He says follow me! Out of the darkness, and into His light. And you continue to carry that light. If He goes up the mountain, you go up the mountain. If He goes down into the valley, you go down into the valley. If He comes to the edge of a river and says cross it... you have to step into the river and cross it. He sets the pace. You follow it.

But sometimes, the next step doesn't look safe.

The untimely step

"It was the harvest season, and the Jordan was overflowing its banks" (Joshua 3:15).

Oh boy. "'Cross the river!' He said. 'It'll be great!' He said..."

Remember, when the Israelites finally got to the Jordan River, which were now white water rapids, God told them to consecrate themselves, prepare for a big move of God, and camp out for three days. Some thought that was too long to wait, "Jericho's ready to be conquered *now*! Let's move!" Some thought that wasn't long enough. "Let's at least wait a couple weeks for flood season to pass." The book of Numbers tells us there were over 600,000 registered men when

Joshua started leading, so we're talking about a couple *million* people getting ready to cross a raging river.

The Promised Land is right on the other side. You can see it. But why now? This isn't a path. This isn't a way forward. Maybe you've been following Jesus this whole way, but this just doesn't make sense. This is impossible. Maybe I'm too early. Maybe I'm too late. Maybe I misunderstood God.

When our daughter was finishing first grade, Mike and I (Kelsey) were living with Mike's parents. We occupied an in-law suite above their garage with the kind of cheap rent you only get when your parents are your landlords. That May, I was given a position on staff at our church on the creative team. The offices were an hour away and it took about a week of making that commute to realize two hours every day in the car was not going to work for our family.

We started looking for an apartment in the area near the church offices, but were disheartened to realize the cost of renting in the real world was astronomical. The places listed online that seemed too-good-to-be-true were, in fact, neither true nor good. It seemed like there were more scams than legitimate homes.

One day, Mike drove around town while I looked at apartment listings from the passenger seat. I'd punch one into the GPS, he would drive to the address to see how sketchy the neighborhood was. Everything we could afford was in an unsavory part of town. After driving by the last listing, we worked our way out of town and checked Zillow one more time. Something new popped up! And it was on the road we were driving at that very moment!

It was a duplex that sat on the corner of two streets, one of which led to the parking lot of the elementary school. A cute side yard would allow our daughter space to play. An adorable bay window in the front was simply beckoning a Christmas tree. It was everything we wanted, and we saw it in the perfect narrow window of time.

Because I was now working full time, and Mike was traveling full time with his improv ministry, we could report dual income on our application. No sooner did we apply than we heard back from the landlord, "we're still having the open house and you're invited to come. But you'll notice we took the listing down because we received more applications than we can process." We saw the listing in the mere eight hours it was online. God's timing seemed right on time.

We got the apartment. We were on our own, making a decent living, and loving every bit of it. We remember one fall day strolling home from having walked our daughter to her new school and we thought out loud, "This is it! We've arrived. Life could not get better. Everything we've been through has led to this, and it seems like smooth sailing from here!"

That was the fall of 2019. Before the end of the school year, Mike would be completely without work, and due to budget cuts, my salary would be cut to 80% of what I expected. And we still had rent to pay. Rent, which went from being about 30% of our income to about 90% of our income. All of a sudden, we found ourselves at the raging rapids. Was this the right move? Should we have stayed with Mike's parents? Did we hear God right? This is impossible. This timing is terrible. Why is this happening? How are we going to get through this?

We think these things, don't we? We have these questions in our walk with Jesus. Why am I here? This doesn't make sense. This isn't the right time. Can't I go around?

That's goal-thinking. Remember, when it comes to following God at His pace, the goal is not the goal. What's the goal? The growth is the goal. The process of crossing this river, the faith needed to do it, and the heart that grows through it, are more important right now than getting into the Promised Land.

Remember all the Israelites who saw God split the Red Sea? All those adults died over the past 40 years in the wilderness. So these people at the bank of the Jordan were young, or not yet born at the time. They would have heard the story of the Red Sea, but not many would remember it. God wanted to show a whole new generation what He could do. Bring them to the edge of an impossible obstacle, then demonstrate nothing is impossible for Him. That's what builds their faith. That's the process. They'll need that faith for the upcoming obstacles.

But God was doing something else by crossing this river...

Throwdown at the Jordan

The Jordan River is at flood stage. It's been storming. It's been raining. The river is raging. In the minds of the local Canaanite people, this is the display of the power and provision of their god, Baal. Baal is their god of storms and rain. This flood season is the height of his power, according to them.

So when God rolls up to the bank of the Jordan River, He's taking off his gloves. He's rolling up His sleeves. He's saying, "Let's do this. If your god is anything, let's see him try to stop me."

Remember, the Levites were to lead the people by carrying the Ark of the Covenant into the river. God would go first. *God isn't calling you to follow Him into anything He hasn't already conquered.* So it's fine if He stacks the odds against Himself, because despite what the obstacle looks like, the odds aren't stacked against you!

It feels like they are sometimes, though, doesn't it?

Have you heard the Bible verse, "God doesn't give you anything beyond what you can handle"? Nope, you haven't, because it's not a Bible verse. 1 Corinthians 10:13 assures us God won't let us be tempted beyond what we can handle; thank the Lord! But nowhere does the Bible say God won't give you more than you can handle. In fact, He'll give you more than you can handle *all the time*, because *God doesn't get glory for anything you can handle yourself.*

You know the phrase, "No guts, no glory?" God has no problem growing the obstacles as big as He wants because when it comes to following Jesus, "more guts, *more* glory." And you better remember it's *your* guts, and *His* glory we're talking about. God isn't calling you to follow Him into anything He hasn't already conquered. But you do have to take the scary step.

Are you at a river or a sea?

"As soon as the feet of the priests who were carrying the Ark touched the water at the river's edge... " (Joshua 3:15)

We'll get to the rest of the verse later, but we can't ignore this detail: their feet had to touch the water's edge. I can't overstate how rage-y the Jordan gets during flood season, even today. The edge of the river is not a picnic area. It's not like you could just wade in up to your ankles. Take one step in, and you could be swept away. Not to mention, the Levites were carrying the Ark on long poles, and it was covered in gold. It was heavy. If they touched it, even accidentally, they would die. And now... step into this river? That's a scary step for the people carrying the presence of God!

I'm guessing there were some prayers of negotiation ... "Hey God, remember when you split the Red Sea? Could you do that again? Remember how Moses held up his staff, and the sea split, and everyone walked across? You did it once, you can do it again, God!"

True, He could. But this is different. Forty years ago, standing in front of the impassable barrier of the Red Sea, Egypt was in hot pursuit behind their Hebrew ex-slaves. They couldn't go back. It was certain death. And there was no way forward. So God made a way forward. All Moses had to do was raise his staff. All the people had to do was watch. That's a Red Sea miracle. We like Red Sea miracles.

But here at the Jordan River, at the edge of the Promised Land, who was closing in behind them? Nobody. They could turn around and go back to the life they were used to. They had a choice; they had options. Nobody was behind them. But who was ahead of them? God. God was already ahead of them. They would have to take a risk and *choose* to go forward.

The best is ahead

Let's paint a picture of what "forward" looks like.

As we've said, the story of Joshua isn't primarily about Joshua. It's a story about a God who can neither be stopped nor rushed in delivering on His promises, and who gets elbow-deep into the work of transforming hearts along the way.

The same is true today. Yes, there is a Jordan River raging in front of you. Yes, there is a Jericho ahead of you. Yes, there are battles along the way, but through it all, in His perfect timing, God will equip you to be the person He wants you to be. It's with this in mind that we can confidently say, the best is always ahead of you.

"Mike, Kelsey, how can you *know* that?" We're not saying this because some megachurch pastors say it to inspire their people. We're not saying this because we want you to like us and give this book a five-star review. We're saying the best is ahead, confidently, because *that's how God works*. One hundred percent of the time.

"And I am certain that God, who began the good work within you, will continue his work until it is finally finished on the day when Christ Jesus returns" (Philippians 1:6).

As long as God is working within you, the best is still ahead. And He promises to finish what He started. But that doesn't mean you can go on autopilot. "Great! Thanks, God! Let me know when you're done!" It also doesn't mean you can accomplish it on your own. I know too many tired, disillusioned people who are trying to mold themselves into someone God will accept in the end. "Okay, thanks, God! I got it from here!" You can't accomplish the work yourself, so what is your role? Embrace the pace.

James coaches us in the beginning of his letter, "For you know that when your faith is tested, your endurance has a chance to grow. So let it grow, for when your endurance is fully developed, you will be perfect and complete, needing nothing" (James 1:3-4).

If you're faithful to follow Him through the trials of life, there is always more grace, more blessing, more growth, more purpose. God is never going to say, "Well I hope you enjoyed your first year of being a Christian, because it's all downhill from here." Or, "I hope you enjoyed your first year of marriage, because the honeymoon's over." No! Jesus is the one who turned water into wine at the end of the night, and it was the best wine the wedding planner ever tasted! The best is always ahead.

It sounds weird to say, but God's *best* wasn't even the time when Jesus was on earth. Jesus himself admitted: you're not going to believe this, but it's best for you that I go away, because if I don't, the Holy Spirit won't come (John 16:7). And ultimately, we know the *absolute* best for us is ahead, an eternity without pain or sorrow or shame, for those who acknowledge Jesus as their Lord. The best is always ahead.

This, by the way, is the opposite of what Satan offers. *With Satan, the best is always behind you.* The first time was the best. And you could spend the rest of your life trying to experience the high of that first time, but you'll never reach it. The first hit of drugs. That first night. The first rush. And we're not just talking about sin. Maybe it's the first win. Maybe you miss the golden days. The way life used to be before the big change happened. Whatever it is you're chasing and wishing to get back to, that's not the Promised Land. You're facing a scary river, and you're looking behind you. That's Egypt. You want to go back there because at least it's familiar. You know what you could expect. But did you forget? You were a slave there! You weren't free.

If you don't trust God, you reject the best ahead, and you'll think the best is behind you. You'll want to go back there. If you trust Him to lead you, the best will always be ahead. Don't forget that.

You can't wait until things look safe before you take the next step with Jesus. Is He a comforter? Yes. Is He a protector? Yes. Are you safe with Him? Absolutely. But that doesn't mean the situation around you is going to *look* safe. He's the one who walks with you through the valley of the shadow of death. He doesn't turn it into Rainbow Unicorn Valley. He's the one who held Peter's hand as he walked on the stormy sea. He didn't calm the sea before Peter stepped out of the boat. But we're over here, praying things like "God, take the temptation away." "God, fix this financial situation." "God, heal me first." "God, make it so these people aren't so negative around me." And then we're discouraged when those things don't happen.

Give me a sign!

We're used to signs telling us where to go ahead of time. Exit 5, half-mile ahead. Chick-fil-A, ten miles ahead. But here's the tough reality about the road to the Promised Land: *God doesn't usually give signs before you take your step of faith.* With God, the signs usually come after. Not always, but usually. We look back, and He confirms that our faith was well-placed. He also knows we so easily doubt. Even if He gave us a sign, we might doubt if it's really from God. So usually, God calls us to take the first step, and then He'll show the signs of what He's been up to.

Besides, why give Israel a sign ahead of time when He already promised them what would happen? Prior to crossing the river, God already said, "As soon as their feet touch the water, the flow of water will be cut off" (Joshua 3:13).

> **YOU CAN'T WAIT UNTIL THINGS LOOK SAFE BEFORE YOU TAKE THE NEXT STEP WITH JESUS.**

"Well, Mike, if God already told them what would happen, shouldn't it be easy to do it?" I don't know. You tell me:

- Jesus said in Matthew 6:33, "Seek the kingdom first (that means prioritize building the church, discipling others, sharing the gospel), and God will meet all your other needs, so you don't have to worry." He already told you what will happen. Does that make it easy? Does that stop you from worrying about how bills will get paid? Does that inspire you to actually start that thing God put on your heart to do? I surely hope so. But it can still be scary. Step anyway. You don't need a sign.

- Paul wrote in Philippians 4:6-7: "Don't worry about anything. Instead, pray about everything. Tell him what you need and thank him for what you have. Then you will experience God's peace." God already told you what will happen. If you pray about everything, and thank Him for what He's done, then you will experience God's peace. God already told you what will happen. So now, do you pray about everything? *Everything?* Big and small? Before you worry about it, not as a last resort? Do you tell Him what you need and thank Him for what you have? He already promised to give you peace. Does it still feel risky? Ideally, no, but yes—sometimes it does.

- John penned in 1 John 1:9: "If we confess our sins, he is faithful and just and will forgive us our sins and purify us from all unrighteousness." If you confess your sin, God promises to forgive you and purify your heart from that sin. He promised it. You don't need a sign that He'll forgive you. But repenting is not a one-time thing. Do you have anything you're afraid to confess and give up? Are you afraid you've messed up too much? Afraid of failing again? Lies. God has promised. The ball is in your court. What are you going to do about it?

God had promised Israel lots of things would happen. That's why they were even here in the first place. He told them He would take them into the Promised Land. But the generation prior to this group at the river's edge still worried and wanted to turn back. So God, in essence, stood there at the river's edge with them, and said to them like He would say to you, "I'm making you a promise. If you want to experience the joy of what lies ahead, you're going to have to believe me, and take the steps you need to take. I know it looks scary. But I already gave you my promise. You don't need another sign."

And so... they got risky, and stepped into the river. And then...

The water above that point began backing up a great distance away at a town called Adam, which is near Zarethan. And the water below that point flowed on to the Dead Sea until the riverbed was dry. Then all the people crossed over near the town of Jericho.

Meanwhile, the priests who were carrying the Ark of the Lord's Covenant stood on dry ground in the middle of the riverbed as the people passed by. They waited there until the whole nation of Israel had crossed the Jordan on dry ground (Joshua 3:16-17).

The miracle upstream

The water was stopped upstream, piled up in a heap a great distance away. While Israel was standing on the bank of the river, probably a bit nervous at the idea of stepping into it, *God already performed the miracle upstream!* They just hadn't seen it yet.

This is so cool. While you're standing here worrying about what will happen, it could be that God already started the miracle a great distance away. And you'll see the effects of it when you get risky and take that first scary step.

Some people who try to explain the Bible without God (which, by the way, is like trying to explain the Gettysburg Address while pretending Abraham Lincoln didn't exist) will say, "it's common for landslides to occur in that region of Israel. These landslides can dam the river and completely cut it off downstream for extended periods of time." Okay. I'll grant that as a possibility. But let's consider this:

In Matthew 17:24-27, we read about what seems like a supernatural event. Jesus was being accused of not paying the temple tax. After making an argument that citizens of heaven don't need to pay taxes to God's house, He ultimately decided this wasn't the hill for Him to die on, so He instructed Peter to do what Peter did well, and go fishing. The first fish he caught held a coin in its mouth, the exact amount for the temple tax.

Did the coin materialize in the fish's mouth as soon as Peter looked inside? No one knows, but I doubt it. I imagine a hungry fish could have snatched up the shiny, but inedible, morsel from a number of situations: a merchant meets a fisherman on the docks, and a coin slips from his grip as he pays the man for his day's catch. A seagull snatches something shiny from the market, and accidentally drops it over the lake. A wistful young man launches a coin as far as he can into the water, hoping to receive luck and favor with the pretty girl selling flowers.

What if someone, in an attempt to deny the existence of God, could prove the origin of that coin? Would an explanation of that scenario make Peter's catch less miraculous? Is it any less of a miracle if God chooses to use natural events with supernatural timing? No, because Jesus knew exactly what was needed, when it was needed, and He arranged for it to have maximum impact for the benefit of those He wanted to reach. That's a miracle.

And while I believe God can do—and does—the impossible and inexplicable today, I think we do ourselves a disservice by defining a miracle as something that can't be explained. Atheists attempt to weaken the faith of Christians by providing potential explanations for miracles in the Bible. As if by identifying the science behind an event, one could remove the need for the divine. And anything that can't be explained now, they would say, will be explained later when science and technology advances to be able to observe more. You know what?

Maybe they're right. Maybe science could explain *what* happens. But it can never explain *why* it happens.

Johannes Kepler was a German astronomer at the turn of the 17th century. He said, "Science is thinking God's thoughts after him." Science can only discover what God already thought to do. It observes the systems and details God set in motion from creation. Sometimes, it might be able to discover how God broke the expectations to do something previously unheard of, what we might call a miracle. But why did God do it? And why did He choose this way instead of another way? And why now instead of earlier or later? Those are questions we have to submit to the fact that He is God and we are not.

This conversation matters in your struggle to embrace God's pace as you hope for miraculous breakthroughs in your life. There's a big difference between expecting God will perform a miracle, and expecting what a miracle would look like. In our seasons of financial drought, I expected God to provide through a big, unexpected check in the mail, because I heard stories of that happening, and I wanted the instant relief it would provide. Instead, we received one smaller, anonymous donation through someone at church, an extra gig we weren't expecting, another paid project, a handful of free groceries, and a couple well-timed deals on things we had to buy. And who knows what sorts of would-be-surprise medical, automobile, or household bills God spared us from in that season? Should I be ungrateful and discontent because I didn't see "my miracle"?

Let God do what God does, how God wants to do it, and when God wants to do it. Your responsibility is to obey. Like Peter, put your line in the water. Like the priests carrying the ark, step into the river.

"Mike, Kelsey, one more thing."

We're trying to wrap up this chapter, but okay, what's on your mind?

"What if the priests didn't step into the river? God had already started the miracle upstream."

Honestly, I don't know. I don't know what would have happened. But I know what *wouldn't* have happened. They wouldn't have trusted God, they wouldn't have seen this victory, and God wouldn't have been glorified. Maybe it's best they didn't find out, and obeyed instead.

Like I said earlier, this wasn't the Red Sea. They had the choice. You have the same choice. Do you step forward into where God is leading you? Or do you step back into what has been comfortable or familiar? It may feel risky to step ahead when God calls you forward. It's even riskier to step backward.

Chapter Five

The Memorial

We get so energized when we finally reach the other side of the obstacle that's been in our way, right? God did this amazing thing to overcome this impossible obstacle! Isn't that exciting and empowering? God does something amazing in your life, something you've been waiting for weeks, months, years—praise God—and you want to just charge ahead and make up for lost time!

That's goal thinking. Remember, the goal isn't the goal. The growth is the goal.

You want to get to Jericho? Yeah, me too! But God's plan and God's pace is higher and better than ours. If it was up to us, we might reach goals all the time (as people certainly do), but we wouldn't be the kind of people God wants us to be. This life isn't about doing things for God. It's about being people of God. And do people of God do things? Absolutely, but we do things so that through the process of doing them, we become more like Jesus.

To finally cross the threshold into the Promised Land after all these years, God held back millions of gallons of raging river water to allow millions of his people to cross on dry ground. I'm sure this took all day. The ones who crossed first were probably itching to get into the

Promised Land. "Let's send our fighters ahead and take Jericho! The women and the kids can keep crossing the river." But even after crossing the river, the process isn't done. Even after an amazing miracle, the goal isn't the goal.

When all the people had crossed the Jordan, the Lord said to Joshua, "CHARGE!!!"—no. He said this:

> "Now choose twelve men, one from each tribe. Tell them, 'Take twelve stones from the very place where the priests are standing in the middle of the Jordan. Carry them out and pile them up at the place where you will camp tonight.'" So Joshua called together the twelve men he had chosen—one from each of the tribes of Israel. He told them, "Go into the middle of the Jordan, in front of the Ark of the Lord your God. Each of you must pick up one stone and carry it out on your shoulder—twelve stones in all, one for each of the twelve tribes of Israel. We will use these stones to build a memorial." (Joshua 4:1-6)

Before you rush on to the next thing, before you tackle the next obstacle, remember to remember. Don't forget to not forget. Build a memorial.

We mostly use memorials to honor someone who died. That's not what this is about. When God shows up and does something amazing, you're going to tell yourself, "I'll never forget this!" And hey, maybe you won't, but do you want to make *sure* you never forget it? Make a memorial. Save something. Make something. Paint something. Write something. Whatever it takes. The reality is life will go on. Satan will distract you and make you doubt the details of your memory. Why does Satan want you to forget? Because *remembering what God did is how you build your faith for the next obstacle.*

Here's a serious question to consider: *how has God shown up in your life?*

Think about it and answer it for yourself right now. If the best you can do is a generic, "Well, He's been good, I guess. I've got a job and a house and a nice family..." Well, that's nice, but what are you going to do when something happens to that job or house or family? Then what? What do you have? How has God shown up in your life, specifically? When did He do something only He can do? When specifically did you experience His peace or provision or protection?

We have a few different kinds of "memorials" throughout our house, but the one that holds the most memories is a jar filled with a few trinkets that represent our time leading a small group Bible study. Over the course of about three years with that group, we saw God do some amazing things.

I look at this memorial jar, and I remember Rachel. She felt trapped by a toxic, abusive boss and workplace. She wanted to quit, but she was scared to quit without another job offer on the table. A new job was Rachel's Promised Land, but God wasn't going to simply scoop her up and drop her into it. The process was too important. We prayed with her as she finally took the risky step to jump without seeing a net. Sure enough, God caught her and gave her a wonderful job in another state (which was a bonus nod to her heart's desire to travel. God loves blessing His children with more than they ask for).

I look at this memorial jar, and I remember Jinhai. He was a Buddhist and an atheist, and he visited us on the recommendation of

Kelsey's brother, who is both a Christian and a respected scientist. Jinhai was curious to know how you could believe in Jesus and trust science at the same time. He ended up giving his life to Christ.

I look at this memorial jar, and I remember Candace. We prayed for her dad to recover from brain cancer. God didn't answer our prayers the way we hoped, but the strength and peace God brought to that family in the wake of his passing was undeniable.

I look at this memorial jar, and I remember not one, but *two* young men in the group who are no longer with us. Trent was a gifted chef, and some of our favorite evenings were when we brought some of his favorite pastries. But one night, he fell asleep at the wheel and crashed through a guardrail over a river. Jack was an ambulance driver, and succumbed to a disease he contracted on the job. Jack's mother will still tell us that this small group was the first and only place where Jack felt like he had friends, where people were kind to him.

We saw God provide jobs, heal diseases, save pregnancies, and revive marriages. We wrote answers to prayer on little black stones and saved them in this memorial jar. My only regret is that we didn't write more, because remembering what God did is how you build your faith for the next obstacle.

But wait, there's more!

Joshua also set up another pile of twelve stones in the middle of the Jordan, at the place where the priests who carried the Ark of the Covenant were standing. And they are there to this day.

The priests who were carrying the Ark stood in the middle of the river until all of the Lord's commands that Moses had given to Joshua were carried out. Meanwhile, the people hurried across the riverbed.

And when everyone was safely on the other side, the priests crossed over with the Ark of the Lord as the people watched (Joshua 4:9-11).

Did you catch that? Another memorial! The twelve representatives already took their stones and carried them across to the other side. We'll see that memorial built in a minute. But Joshua went to the middle of the river and built another memorial *in the middle of the river*.

Why two? Why there? What good will that do?

One autumn morning in 2013, I (Mike) woke up with a splitting headache. Normally, I'd stay in bed and try to sleep it off, but I was in a hotel in Philadelphia, and I had to catch a flight home. I barely remember getting up and out the door. Fortunately, I was traveling with my improv group, so I didn't have to drive. I stumbled through security and finally got to my gate. I sprawled out on an uncomfortable airport chair, barely conscious. Later, my companions said other travelers were walking by and looking at me either concerned or judgmental, or both, "It's six in the morning, and he's already that drunk?"

I don't remember getting home and heading straight to bed, but I do remember trying to sleep off the headache, without success. After a few hours, I emerged from my room to prove to Kelsey I was still alive.

She interrupted me, "Wait a minute. Look at me. Open your eyes."

"I am."

"That's as much as your right eye can open?"

"Um... yeah, I guess so..."

"We're going to the hospital."

At the emergency room, the staff took me in to run some tests.

They warned Kelsey, "It's tough to tell right now, but it's possible he has bacterial meningitis. We have to take him to the emergency room."

"Aren't we at the emergency room?!"

"No, this is urgent care." We'd never done this before; we didn't know where to go! It was an emergency, and this was a room! How were we supposed to know? Before I knew it, they loaded me into my first ambulance ride. In fact, I was too in-and-out of consciousness to know anything. At the *actual* hospital, they ran more tests and brought Kelsey the news: Your husband has a pituitary tumor. Honestly, that was a relief to Kelsey at that point. Bacterial meningitis can kill you in hours. This was still an emergency surgery situation, but it was less of, well, an emergency. You know it's a rough day when you're thankful for a tumor.

This is when we saw God starting to line things up. One of the nation's leading pituitary surgeons was at that hospital, and had availability that day. They prepped me for surgery, and this is where I have to let Kelsey tell her side of the story, because I was completely unconscious moving forward.

Mike was laying in a bed in a bit of a holding room before surgery. I (Kelsey) made all sorts of arrangements. I went home and packed an overnight bag. I found friends to take care of our daughter, who had just turned one. I called family members to give them the news and updates. Back in Mike's room, there was nothing else I could do but wait.

A nurse entered the room with a smile almost as bright as her white scrubs. While two other orderlies came to roll Mike's bed out of the room, she came over to me, put her hands on my shoulders, and said, "Everything's okay, baby. He's gonna be fine." It felt more comforting than the typical nurse bedside manner. I felt like it *truly* was going to be okay, and I felt the anxiety leave my body.

The nurse continued, "They're gonna move him to another room. Can I take your overnight bag? I'll keep it at the nurse's station so you can come get it when you need it." I agreed, so the nurse left with the bag, and the others transported Mike to another room.

I was so relaxed after the encouragement from the nurse, in fact, that when my brother came to the hospital to support me, he expected to come in and find me crying and upset, but instead found me asleep in the waiting room! Just like Jesus sleeping in the boat during the storm, when you trust God, He gives you peace that doesn't make sense.

After the surgery, Mike had to spend a couple nights in the ICU, as protocol for that procedure. I went back to get our overnight bag from the nurse's station. The nurse I talked to earlier wasn't at the desk, so I asked these nurses if they could bring out my bag.

"Sorry, we don't have any bags back here."

I explained my interaction with the other nurse and what she had told me to do.

These nurses raised their eyebrows. "Wait. Can you describe the nurse you talked to?"

"Yeah, she's *really* tall. Dark skin, really pretty. Gold ribbons in her hair? White scrubs." I can't overstate how gorgeous this nurse was.

"Nobody on our staff fits that description..." The nurses on duty looked concerned.

"Okay... well... she said she would put the bag behind the nurse's station. Can you just check and see?"

They did. A few seconds later, they emerged from a room behind the nurse's station, rolling our luggage behind them, a bit baffled. "Well, sure enough. Is this your bag?"

"Yes! Thanks!" I collected my bag and joined Mike in the room where he would soon wake up.

Kelsey and I (Mike; I'm awake now) ended up telling this story to our small group at the time, and our friend Candace (who I mentioned earlier from our memorial jar) heard Kelsey describe the mystery nurse.

"Yeah, I've never seen that nurse either. Wait—you said she wore white scrubs?"

"Definitely white."

"That's impossible."

You see, Candace's dad had been battling brain cancer for months. Candace visited that same hospital, on that same floor of the brain care unit, every day.

She explained, "That hospital color-codes their scrubs. Each unit has its own color, for safety reasons. White scrubs wouldn't be allowed on that unit. In fact, I don't think there are white scrubs in the entire hospital."

We believe, what maybe you've suspected as I've told the story, Kelsey met an angel who was sent to bring peace. And sure enough, the angel nurse was right; the surgery was a success.

But there were two more obstacles in front of us. First, most patients who have a pituitary tumor the size of mine need to have hormone replacement therapy for the rest of their life. Daily pills provide the hormones that the now-damaged pituitary gland can't produce. I got tested, and the endocrinologist invited me in to discuss the results.

He said, "I talk with people after this surgery all the time. I've worked with your surgeon for years. And this is the first time I've been able to say to someone that your hormone levels are perfect, and you don't need to see me again." Medically, it was as if the tumor never happened.

Financially, though, it was a different story. The second obstacle was the fact that we didn't have health insurance. Nothing. Have you ever wondered what paying for brain surgery out of pocket looks like? I kept one of the bills. $53,464. And four cents. The extra four cents felt insulting, frankly.

That was just the surgery and hospital stay. If you add on top of that the ambulance ride, the scans, and the tests, our total bill was close to $70,000. It might as well have said three gazillion dollars. It was an impossible obstacle for us. A raging river we simply could not cross.

We applied for some financial aid. Maybe there would be something available to help with a payment plan. Two weeks later, we got a letter stating our request for aid had been approved, to the total of *one hundred percent* of the bill. All of it. Covered in full.

Well, after our co-pay of $35. Deal.

I've kept these papers, the original bill, the hormone test results, and the financial aid letter, as a memorial. Because God did something amazing that month. And He deserves better than for me to forget that He did it. *But it's not just about remembering what God did. It's about remembering what God can do.*

Remember, Joshua put up a memorial in the middle of the river. Soon, the water would come crashing back down, and cover it up. Why the middle of the river? Because there would be one time a year when you could actually see this memorial. In the drought season, when the water is low, when life is more of a struggle to get by... that's when you could see this memorial. That's when you can remember what God did.

When I, or someone in my family is sick, I can see these papers and remember that God is a healer. Our finances have never been a steady stream. We have flood seasons and drought seasons. And sometimes the drought seasons are long and hard. I can look at these papers and remember that God doesn't care how many digits are in front of the decimal point. And I can't minimize or exaggerate the impact in my mind, because the memorial is there.

In the drought, I have a constant reminder that God is good, He's in control, and my story isn't about me. It's about Him.

But this memorial isn't even just for me. Check this out...

> The Lord had said to Joshua, "Command the priests carrying the Ark of the Covenant to come up out of the riverbed." So Joshua gave the command. As soon as the priests carrying the Ark of the Lord's Covenant came up out of the riverbed and their feet were on high ground, the water of the Jordan returned and overflowed its banks as before. (Joshua 4:16-18)

By the way, remember how God was the first one into the river, by the Ark of the Covenant going first? God was the first one in, and He's the last one out. God goes ahead of you and He goes behind you. Don't you dare think you're on this journey alone. But let's keep reading:

The people crossed the Jordan on the tenth day of the first month. Then they camped at Gilgal, just east of Jericho. It was there at Gilgal that Joshua piled up the twelve stones taken from the Jordan River.

> Then Joshua said to the Israelites, "In the future your children will ask, 'What do these stones mean?' Then you can tell them, 'This is where the Israelites crossed the Jordan on dry ground.' For the Lord your God dried up the river right before your eyes, and he kept

it dry until you were all across, just as he did at the Red Sea when he dried it up until we had all crossed over. He did this so all the nations of the earth might know that the Lord's hand is powerful, and so you might fear the Lord your God forever." (Joshua 4:19-24)

The memorial wasn't just there for those who experienced the miracle. The memorial was there as a conversation starter for people who need to believe in something they didn't see.

It's your physical testimony.

It's a conversation starter.

It's on your desk at work. "Hey what's that thing?" "Oh man, great story. You won't believe what God did."

It's on your shelf. "Daddy, what's that for?" "Oh, sweetie, let me tell you how God took care of us."

Memories store feelings. Memorials build faith.

If what God did only lives in your mind, you're going to have to fight feelings with feelings in the rough seasons, and that's a hard fight.

If you have a physical memorial of what God did, in the rough seasons, you have something you can point to and say "it doesn't matter how I feel now; I only have this because God showed up, and He can do it again." Make it physical. It's not just here in Joshua.

MEMORIES STORE FEELINGS. MEMORIALS BUILD FAITH.

1 Samuel 7, after God wiped out the Philistines, Samuel made a memorial and called it Ebenezer, which means Stone of Help, saying "Up to this point, God has helped us!" And you better believe that memorial built their faith to know that God will continue to help.

Genesis 28, God appeared to Jacob and promised Jacob that the very ground he was sleeping on would be given to his descendants. This was literally the Promised Land. Jacob was overwhelmed that God would meet with him here, and he set up a memorial called "Bethel," which means "House of God", saying "the Lord is in this place, and I didn't even know it!" And now, when his descendants come back to the Promised Land, they can know "This is God's house!"

You want a New Testament example of a memorial? If you've been to church in the past month, you've likely observed one. Communion, or the Lord's Supper, is a memorial Jesus built for our sake. Jesus said "eat this bread" and "drink this cup"—in what?—"in remembrance of me." It's a physical reminder of what Jesus did, and we can look forward to Him coming back.

Let communion be a conversation starter. Your kid might be sitting next to you, and they may ask, "Why are you having snacks?" And you can say, "oh, it's not a snack. We don't eat this because we're hungry. We eat this because it's how we remember that Jesus died as a punishment for our sins, so we don't have to be punished."

What else has Jesus done in your life?

What do you have to remind yourself about it? What do you have that others can see and ask about? Remembering what God has done is how you build faith for the future.

Chapter Six

The Downtime

News about the new neighbors spread like wildfire. Not even the raging Jordan River, Baal's mighty eastern barrier, could keep Israel and their God out of Canaan. When the Amorite and Canaanite kings heard how the Jordan River dried up to allow the Israelites to cross, "they lost heart and were paralyzed with fear because of them" (Joshua 5:1).

What a prime time to strike! The enemies would be willing to practically hand over their cities!

And haven't the Israelites waited long enough? Haven't they done enough of the "process"? They consecrated themselves. They crossed the river. They even took time to build some rock piles like God told them to. Now they're here. It's time to move forward and go on the offensive before their enemies regain their courage. There's no retreat now that the river has returned to normal behind them. The longer they wait, the more danger they'll be in, right? Time to move!

Joshua awaited God's orders. He was ready to lead the charge. He could picture the fear on the faces of the Amorite Kings. Victory was close; he could smell it.

Then God spoke.

"Make flint knives, and—"

Yes! Joshua must have thought. *We'll slice the throats of the enemy kings! Blood will be spilt in the name of Yahweh our God!*

"—circumcise this second generation of Israelites."

I'm sorry—what? Circumcise? I think I heard you wrong. You must have said "serve supplies?"... "send some spies?"

Circumcise this entire group of Israelites? No man in the past forty years since leaving Egypt had been circumcised. This meant every man of fighting age had to undergo this sensitive, crippling surgery—on the doorstep of the enemy!

But this shouldn't have surprised anyone. This was God's expectation of His people ever since He called the first father of the nation, Abraham:

> This is the covenant that you and your descendants must keep: Each male among you must be circumcised... Your bodies will bear the mark of my everlasting covenant. Any male who fails to be circumcised will be cut off from the covenant family for breaking the covenant. (Genesis 17:10, 13-14)

In other words—and please forgive me if this sounds crass, but I believe God intended the wordplay—cut it off, or be cut off. Let's not downplay how serious God was about His people's part in keeping this covenant. Even after God commissioned Moses to free His people from Egypt, God was willing to *kill* Moses over the fact that he had not yet kept the covenant by circumcising his son (Exodus 4:24-26). This alone should warn us that God is more concerned about our obedience than our ministry. Many Christians have pursued a ministry because of their love of God. Sadly, too many of them have fallen from favor because they lost their fear of God. *A fear of God keeps you where your love of God carries you.*

Back to Joshua. On one of their many long walks together, Moses had probably told him about the day God almost killed him for not circumcising his son. Joshua wasted no time in relaying this command to the people. And while I'm sure nobody was excited about it, they obeyed.

Thank God, today, we can read Paul's letters to the Christians in Rome and Galatia, and see clearly that God doesn't demand circumcision now that Jesus has come. But what He expected physically of His people before Jesus, He's expecting of our *hearts* today.

"...true circumcision is not merely obeying the letter of the law; rather, it is a change of heart produced by the Spirit" (Romans 2:29).

A change of heart

With this in mind, let's consider some of the lessons Joshua and the people learned through this act of obedience. Let's also reflect on how we can be obedient to this "change of heart produced by the Spirit" today.

#1: Being Dependent

When I was lying in the hospital bed after my brain surgery, there wasn't much for me to do. I could read for a short while, pray... and that's about it. The list was short. If you've ever had to recover from surgery, you can relate. It's humbling, needing to rely on the nursing staff to help you with basic functions. There's nothing like lying flat in a hospital bed to convince you that you need to slow down and ask for help.

"After all the males had been circumcised, they rested in the camp until they were healed" (Joshua 5:8). An adult could take up to two weeks to fully recover from this surgery. But don't forget, they had already crossed the Jordan River, and were in *enemy territory!* Their act of obedience left them at their weakest and most vulnerable. And they didn't even have bags of frozen peas to ease their discomfort.

How is God calling you to obey today? Maybe, like the Israelites, there's an expectation, boundary, or righteousness that you haven't kept in a while. The thought of picking it up again is uncomfortable, maybe foreign. The timing doesn't seem right. It doesn't seem safe. It would be painful.

Often, obedience to God puts you in a vulnerable position. Someone could take advantage of you. You could miss opportunities. You could lose income. You could lose reputation. You may get hurt. If you put off your obedience long enough, God may allow you to end up in this position against your will.

But God protects. Just like God wanted to teach the Israelites that their safety didn't come from able-bodied men, He wants to check what you depend on. In these vulnerable positions, you learn that you weren't actually as strong as you thought. You don't *become* vulnerable; you *recognize* your vulnerability. You recognize what you have been depending on—your money, your health, your strength, your intellect, your connections—can be lost in one bad day. You are no less dependent on God on a good day than you are on a bad day; the only difference is whether or not you recognize it.

#2: Being Detached

My social media feed will sometimes resurface memories from to-day's date in previous years. Often it's nostalgic. "That was a great vacation." "Oh, that's funny, I forgot Addy said that when she was three." Every once and a while, though, I'm offered a less-welcome reminder. "Oh… that friendship fell apart painfully." "I'd rather forget that job." Not all memories are worth saving. Tattoos are covered up, once-cherished souvenirs are thrown out, even entire rooms and homes are renovated to put a painful past behind, and usher in a new chapter.

God saw a major distinction between Israel's life in Egypt, and the new life in the Promised Land, and He wanted them to recognize it, too. So He commemorated the occasion with a joke:

"Then the Lord said to Joshua, 'Today I have rolled away the shame of your slavery in Egypt.' So that place has been called Gilgal to this day" (Joshua 5:9).

You see, God is doing some more wordplay here, using the act of circumcision as a metaphor for removing the stigma of the past. *Gilgal* means "rolling", so the Heavenly Dad joke probably had some of them *gilgal* on the floor, laughing.

But seriously, God is in the business of rolling away the past, and starting new futures for His people. To a crippled man, Jesus said, "Roll up your mat and walk" (Matthew 9:6). To the people mourning at Lazarus' tomb, He said, "Roll away the stone" (John 11:39). And, in the ultimate act of *gilgal*, Jesus walked out of His own tomb as the stone was rolled away.

What has God rolled away in your life? Here's your responsibility: don't hang on to what God rolls away. He wants to detach you from the shame and guilt of the past. The more a part of you it feels, the more painful it may be.

#3: Being Distinct

This circumcision was another reminder that God cares more about His people looking different, acting different, listening to Him, and obeying Him than He cares about them reaching their goal. Circumcision is what God asked of Israel, to be an outward symbol representing the inward difference of their hearts.

Is your heart different from the world around you? Because there's a lot of people doing things in Jesus' name. You might say, "I'm going to start this organization for Jesus." "I'm going to preach the gospel, and evangelize in Jesus' name." "I'm going to write a book about Jesus." "I'm going to raise a Christian family." Great. Those are all great goals. And with enough effort, you could very well reach those goals. But there are a lot of people doing a lot of damage because they're doing something in Jesus' *name*, but not with Jesus' *heart*.

IF YOU WANT TO MAKE A DIFFERENCE FOR JESUS, LET JESUS CRAFT YOU A DIFFERENT HEART.

If you want to make a difference for Jesus, let Jesus craft you a different heart. Like the incapacitated Israelite men experienced, it's a long, painful process. It requires making decisions nobody else would make on their own. It requires putting obedience over comfort. It requires waiting.

But waiting is what all of God's closest friends have in common:

Even after *Paul* was saved, dramatically and unmistakably, he lived in the desert for 3 years before starting his ministry, just him and God. No preaching, no writing, no planting churches.

Joseph waited 13 years for his dream to become a reality, many of which were spent in prison. Talk about a painful process.

David waited 15 years *after* he was anointing king, until he actually sat on the throne. Fifteen years of serving the current king with humility, and running for his life while that same king was jealous of him and wanted to kill him.

Abraham waited 25 years for God to fulfill His promise of son, and *never* got to witness the fulfillment of the promise of a great nation.

Moses led sheep in the wilderness for 40 years before he led God's people to—but never *into*—the promised land.

How long are you willing to wait for God to give you a heart that is distinctly His?

Chapter Seven

The Feast

Let's jump forward in time to explore a story found in Luke 17:11-19.

North of Judea, the center of Israel's cultural pride and joy, lay two other regions that were technically also Israel, but nobody in Judea cared to admit it. Directly north was Samaria, a region of cultural and religious half-breeds despised by anyone of pure Jewish heritage. North of Samaria was Galilee, the low-class home of Israel's poorest and hillbilly-est, on the fringe of Jewish life.

On the border of these two dismissed regions sat a small village. Condemned to the outskirts of even this tiny marginalized town, sat ten men. These men had been agonizing for years, afflicted by leprous skin that left them spurned by society, disfigured, and without hope. Hopeless, that is, until they overheard rumors that the miracle worker, Jesus, was headed to their village.

When they spied Jesus' signature small crowd coming up the road, they kept a safe distance, but eagerly tried to get the Messiah's attention.

"Jesus! Master! Have mercy on us!" they waved their pestilence-battered hands in the air.

Jesus smiled and waved back. "Go show yourselves to the priests!"

Is that a yes? That must be a yes! Are you healed yet? Not yet. Are you? Not yet. Well, he said go to the priests! Let's go!

In an act that had been off-limits until now, all ten lepers hobbled toward the village. As they went, they looked at each other and discovered they were all healed! They laughed and cheered and hugged each other, patting their freshly-clean skin. Their walk escalated to a run as they all hurriedly searched for a priest to confirm their new life as healthy, accepted citizens. All, that is, except one.

One man, still smiling from ear to ear, felt his miraculously smooth arms, nose, and fingers. He paused and watched his companions cheerily run ahead into the village. He looked down and cradled his left hand in his right, and a tear fell from his cheek. A glance backward turned into a step backward. A step turned into a run back toward Jesus, and his tears streamed freely.

"Praise God! Praise God!" He shouted as loud as he could muster, and collapsed at the feet of Jesus. "Thank you! Thank you!"

Jesus knelt down. "Praise God indeed! Tell me, where are you from?"

"Samaria," the man responded vaguely, shamefully.

"Well, my Samarian friend, let me ask you another question."

The man looked up to give his attention.

"Didn't I heal ten men?"

A soft nod.

"Then where are the other nine?"

The man couldn't utter an answer, but Jesus didn't need one as He raised His voice and His stature to address the crowd, "Has no one returned to give glory to God except this foreigner?" He smiled down at the man. "Stand up and go. Your faith has healed you."

A question that seems to be on God's mind, and should therefore be on ours, is "What will you do when you receive the thing you've been hoping to receive for so long?" When the river is crossed. When the goal is in sight. When God steps in to miraculously remove the obstacles that had dashed your hopes. What's next?

t's easy to say good riddance to the past, and charge forward like nine former-lepers on their way to start a new life. And certainly, the scorn, the pain, and the depression of the past can certainly be left behind. But not everything in the past ought to be forgotten.

You see, God had another reason to not send His people charging into battle on this side of the river. If God had given them the green light to attack, they would be too busy securing a victory to stop and remember what God had done. We're not talking about the memorial stones at the river. Further back than that. God orchestrated Israel's downtime at Gilgal to offer an opportunity to celebrate and commemorate the victory He secured decades ago. After the worst of the circumcision pain had subsided, but before the men could jump back into the fray, God pointed at the calendar.

"While the Israelites were camped at Gilgal on the plains of Jericho, they celebrated Passover on the evening of the fourteenth day of the first month" (Joshua 5:10).

Passover was a yearly celebration (a memorial, even) to remember God's power and faithfulness in rescuing them from Egypt. At the beginning of every year, Israel took a week to do, in essence, what the tenth leper did: pause, look back at the One who gave new life, and praise God in gratitude and celebration.

Celebration is a concept that is sadly the first to get overlooked in favor of the most recent victory. It's easy to skip what's important when you're starting something new. You can understand why. Pausing feels like waiting (ew, gross, right?). Looking back feels like moving backward.

But here's something the tenth leper demonstrated, and what God reminded Joshua and the people: *Celebration is worship!*

Shine attention to what God has done! Remember His faithfulness! Stand in awe of the power, the wisdom, and the sovereignty with which He won the victories of the distant or recent past. Let the celebration of His accomplishments build your faith to trust that He can do even greater things in the future.

CELEBRATION IS WORSHIP!

Yes, celebration necessitates pumping the breaks on your next conquest. It may mean a downshift in productivity. It will cost something: time, money, momentum. But whose time, money, and momentum are you spending, really? Celebration requires giving back to God what He has already given you, to remember what He has already done for you.

If you're a forward-thinking goal-crusher, and celebration doesn't come easily to you, don't wait for God to carve a space in your calendar for you. Embrace His pace now. God's timing will always include time to celebrate and rest. And don't be surprised if His timing appears dangerously inconvenient.

This celebration in hostile territory reminds me of a line in one of the most famous songs in the world:

"You prepare a feast for me in the presence of my enemies" (Psalm 23:5).

At the intersection of this timeless psalm and this almost-footnote of Joshua's story is where we discover the heart of God reaching out to us in the midst of our scary, impossible obstacles.

God wants to be with you. And He's choosing *this* time and place because He wants you to become the kind of person who is comfortable sitting with Him anywhere. He wants you to learn that *rest is not a waste of time, celebration is not delay, and danger is a matter of perspective.*

If you need to linger on that thought for another minute, please do, but I have to bring attention to the next detail. Also tucked into this easy-to-miss nook of the story are two verses that, to me, are profoundly bittersweet:

"The very next day they began to eat unleavened bread and roasted grain harvested from the land. No manna appeared on the day they first ate from the crops of the land, and it was never seen again. So from that time on the Israelites ate from the crops of Canaan" (Joshua 5:11-12).

Can you imagine? Of the millions of Israelites now entering the Promised Land, only two could have remembered eating anything besides manna and quail: Joshua and Caleb, the two spies who had the faith that God could fulfill his promise. Everyone else was born in the past forty years of desert wandering, or was a mere child in Egypt. The crunch of a vegetable or the sweet juice of a fruit was unknown to this nation of sand people. Every day was the same: wake up early, collect a day's worth of manna (and no more), catch a couple of the many quails around camp, cook, eat, repeat. For forty years. The young generation of Israelites knew nothing else.

Even now, though they were out of the desert and in the early phases of this campaign, manna met them every morning. As they camped by the flooded river, manna. After they crossed and made their stone memorials, manna. As they first recovered from their surgery in Gilgal, manna. The morning before Passover, manna.

Imagine what it would have been like that first morning. You rub your bleary eyes after a not-so-restful sleep. You couldn't help but wonder if the nearby Canaanites had heard the commotion from yesterday's Passover festivities. Apparently not. That's good. In one fluid motion honed by a couple decades of daily routine, your right hand reaches for your gathering basket, and your left hand grabs your cloak from its peg on the tentpole. You're still wrapping your cloak around yourself as you duck and push the tent flap open with your head.

The early rays of the sunrise get your attention. You fix your eyes on the horizon toward Jericho as you stoop down to grab a handful of heaven bread. You've had a complicated relationship with manna. You can't honestly say you *love* it. It lost its novelty a long time ago. You've done your share of complaining about it, about the monotony. But lately… it's hard to describe, but God has been slowly teaching you what it means to be content. To understand His faithfulness doesn't guarantee your comfort. To recognize miracles don't always look like split seas and fiery clouds; sometimes, they look like… wait a minute. Where is it?

You actually look down for the first time this morning and realize a distinct lack of the white flakes dusting the ground to which you've grown accustomed. You look around the camp and hear the commotion of other early risers recognizing the same thing. A few boys run around, excitedly throwing newfound gourds at each other. A nearby woman hesitantly puts a grape in her mouth before her eyes widen in delight. A trio of men victoriously hold a pheasant above their heads.

Watching the dawn of a new season of discovery and plenty, you feel a little sad, and that surprises you. Heaven's daily miracle was gone. You're not ungrateful for the Promised Land, and not worried about where food would come from, but as you cross the threshold into this new phase of life, you're solemnly aware of the fact that from then on, if you're not careful, you might not recognize God's involvement in your daily life like you used to.

Chapter Eight

The Question

The morning of our wedding, my best man invited me out to breakfast. We got up before sunrise and found a diner that served early risers. I wish I could remember any of the conversation, as I'm sure it was encouraging and inspirational, but my mind was whirring with thoughts about the upcoming events of the day. This was my last morning as a single man!

What I *do* remember of that morning was arriving at the church after breakfast. My best man and I prayed, and he left me to sit quietly before entering the venue. I knew, as soon as I stepped foot in the building, I would be on a treadmill of activity. Before that happened, I played a song that has been Track 1 of my "Prayer Playlist" ever since:

> *Before the day slips away,*
> *I want to stop and say I love you.*
> *Before the world rushes in again,*
> *I want to stop and say there's none above you.*
> *I'll just be still and know that you are God.*[2]

Sandwiched between the public, demonstrative events of Israel's first Passover in the Promised Land and the legendary battle of Jericho is a private episode between Joshua and one other man. While short and easy to miss, these four lines of dialogue may be the most important in Joshua's career.

Joshua was walking near the town of Jericho, as we see in Joshua 5:13-15. I imagine a foggy morning. Close enough to sunrise for Joshua to see his way out of the camp and approach the city, but before the sun breached the horizon. The city was cold, closed, restless. It had been on lockdown ever since the spies were reported in the city. Joshua eyed the walls, undoubtedly repeating what God had said to him at the beginning of his new role: "Be strong and courageous." All his prayers, all his preparation, all God's promises... all led to this place.

Can you relate to a moment like this? The morning before a wedding. The hours before a birth. The hallway outside an important meeting room. *There's something special about the time* before *something special*. If you jump into the day, you'll miss it. If you hurry through it, you'll miss it. If you're fixed on the victory itself, you'll miss it. But if you slow your pace and make space for it, there's an eerie, contemplative calm before everything changes.

Wrong question

As Joshua was soaking in this quiet moment and contemplating the calm before the whirlwind of activity he knew was approaching, he was startled to realize he was being watched. He looked up and saw a man standing in front of him. Alarmingly, the man had drawn his sword and was staring straight at him.

Joshua's fight instinct kicked in as he closed the gap. "Friend or foe?" he demanded a response.

"Neither one," the man replied calmly. "I am the commander of the Lord's army."

Joshua was stopped abruptly in his tracks. Almost as quickly as his jaw dropped, he fell facedown to the ground. "I'm at your command. Tell me what you want me to do, and I'll do it."

Let's press pause and sit in the awkwardness of this interaction for a moment. I don't think this is an angel speaking. Angels don't let anyone bow down to worship them. This is God speaking. Quite possibly, it's Jesus himself. Either way, God is speaking. So when Joshua asks, "Are you for us or against us?" God responds, "Wrong question. Neither."

Does that surprise you? We read things like Romans 8:31, "If God is for us, who can be against us?" We sing with Chris Tomlin, "And if our God is for us, then who could ever stop us?!" The drums pound, and we get pumped. We want to charge into the thing in front of us, and we're like, "Yes, let's go! God, are you with me?!"

Wait, wait, wait... we're asking the wrong question. The question is not, "God, are you on my side?" The question is from God who says, "I'm the commander. I'm the one calling the shots."

The *right* question, then, is "Am I on God's side?"

This interaction wasn't a morale boost from which Joshua could go back to his troops and say, "I met with God, and He's with us!". This was a reality check before he rushed into things. We would do well to make sure we're not falling into the trap of thinking we're the main character of the story.

It's easy to think God agrees with us. Politically, theologically. But God doesn't pick sides. Are you on God's side?

The question is more than a clever turn of phrase. What do your prayers sound like? Are you asking God to bless your plan? Is your prayer more like a list of requests you'd like Him to sign off on? If so, it sounds like you might be asking God to follow you. But He asks you to follow Him. And before you charge into the next victory, God wants to know if you're with Him.

The process is the promise

We get a lot of comfort from the idea that God is with us—and rightfully so. It's genuinely encouraging to know that the Creator of the universe is aware of the circumstances of your life, that He cares enough to be involved, and that He's close enough to do something about it. That's why so many resonate with Romans 8:28:

"And we know that God causes everything to work together for the good of those who love God and are called according to his purpose for them."

That's wonderful, but many people cling to that verse and say, "God will work everything out for my good."

"Well isn't that what the verse just said? What's the problem?"

The problem is subtle, but it's revealed with this question: What if your definition of "your good" isn't the same as God's definition? Maybe your prayers are forming an expectation of what you think is good, but God has something else in mind. If you cling to some hope that God will turn your difficult situation into a happier one with more finances and less stress, you'll find yourself approaching God like Joshua initially did, asking God, "Friend or foe?" "Are you with me or are you against me?" "God, I'm up against a wall, and I need to get past this. Are you going to help me or are you going to make this longer and more difficult?"

Wrong question. And you'll miss the point of this verse. First, yes, God works everything out for your good. Amen. It's in the Bible for you, and it's a promise. Second, He's a great and loving God.

Amen. We have a Bible's worth of proof. So, if God is infinitely loving, wouldn't He work everything out for your *greatest* good? Certainly. And what's your *greatest* good? To be like Jesus.

This isn't just an interpretation; it's literally in the next verse. "For God knew his people in advance, and he chose them to become like his Son..." (Romans 8:29, emphasis mine).

To become like His Son. That is the good that God promises to work everything out for. It's a process that God Himself leads, and He will complete it.

We've mentioned Paul's words before and they are worth repeating here. "And I am certain that God, who began the good work within you, will continue his work until it is finally finished on the day when Christ Jesus returns" (Philippians 1:6).

This process of becoming like Jesus won't be complete until we get to heaven, but it promises a life of greater hope, peace, and purpose along the way. The process is the promise.

This study of Joshua is based on a series I taught at our church one summer when our pastor was on sabbatical. Due to the limited number of Sundays I was allotted to teach, I planned on skipping this story of Joshua and the Commander to get into the battle of Jericho.

Isn't that ironic? I was eager to jump to Jericho, celebrate the victories God had done in our lives, and we'd feel happy and end the study on a high. In essence, I was preparing and praying, "God! What a great study this has been! Thanks for this opportunity. Let's go celebrate the victory! Are you with me?!"

But I couldn't get over this unexpected appearance of God in front of Jericho saying, "Wrong question. Are *you* with *me*?"

I took a note from Joshua, knelt face down on the floor in front of my desk, and asked, "What message do you have for your servant?"

And He said, "I want to know if this church is with me."

I didn't know what that meant at the time. I wasn't the pastor of this church! Our pastor's sabbatical was not about soaking up the sun at the beach, but soaking up the vision of what God wanted the church to be. I knew he would return at the end of the summer with a fresh perspective. It wasn't until a couple years later, through hindsight as I browsed my notes to write this book, that I realized what God's question meant.

That summer, our pastor downloaded from God a significant shift for the church in his care. It required him to evaluate his nearly fifty years of theologically Baptist upbringing and lead a twenty-year-old Baptist church into a new era of living as a Bible-based, Spirit-empowered "Word and Spirit" church.

Since then, God has brought about victories in people's lives we had previously thought to be impossible. But unsurprisingly, not everyone was with Him. Some didn't trust the pastor's leadership. Others wanted to keep their religious routines the same as they've always been. Some realized they could no longer keep their pet sins hidden.

WE CAN'T HAVE "GOD WITH US" WITHOUT "GOD LEAD US."

I wish them all grace and mercy wherever they've gone, but this "special time before something special" taught us a valuable lesson: *We can't have "God with us" without "God lead us."* God is with us by leading us. You can't have one relationship with God without the other. Jesus came to be your Shepherd, not to ride shotgun. He's not interested in the passenger seat; He wants to drive. We don't get the Promised Land without the process.

"God, are you with me or not?" Wrong question. More than a friend to agree with you, you need a commander to lead you. The beautiful thing is, when you humbly submit to Jesus' leadership, you become His friend and confidante, too.

As Jesus said, "You are my friends if you do what I command. I no longer call you slaves, because a master doesn't confide in his slaves. Now you are my friends, since I have told you everything the Father told me" (John 15:14-15).

Remove your shoes

Back to Joshua. Joshua humbled himself in front of the Commander of the Lord's Armies and awaited His command. What would it be? Gather the troops? Approach Jericho? Thank goodness, it can't be circumcision again...

"Take off your sandals. You're standing on holy ground."

Sandals? Holy ground? Wait a minute, Joshua had heard this story before. Last time someone said this, it was God speaking to Moses!

Imagine a wrought iron gate at the beginning of a long private driveway. There may even be a security guard posted there, enforcing the rule posted on a sign affixed to the gate, "Private property. Do not enter." If your arrival is expected, you can pass through the gate and drive by dozens of matching topiary bushes lining the driveway as it winds up to the main house. The focal point of the house is a large ornate door. That door, if you're fortunate enough to be invited inside, opens up into a grand foyer. There, you'll be prompted, either by a staff member or by another sign, "Welcome. Please remove your shoes."

For a while, whenever I read "take off your sandals; you're standing on holy ground" in the story of Moses or Joshua, I pictured these two signs at a mansion. I understood "this is holy ground" to imply "no trespassing," and "take off your sandals" to mean "keep your nasty Reeboks off my seven-thousand dollar Persian rug."

But certainly if God wanted Joshua to stay away from holy ground, He would have commanded him to back up. This is an invitation. And we can be confident that God's holiness is not so fragile that someone's dirty sneakers can ruin it. Therefore, I believe the Commander's command to remove his shoes teaches Joshua—and us—two unique lessons in this special moment before something special happens:

Holy ground is God's ground

In *The Mountain in the Desert*, there's an entire chapter devoted to Moses' encounter on holy ground. But this interaction with Joshua is inherently different. There's a reason this encounter occurs near Jericho. God could have met Joshua in his tent, or by the river, or even in a vision. Regardless of where God showed up, it would have been holy ground, and Joshua would have been obligated to remove his shoes. So why here? The ground in front of Jericho, specifically, would soon be trampled by over a million eager Israelites. Before that dirt could get stuck in a single sandal, God claimed it for Himself. This was His battleground. This was the doorstep to His promise. The people were about to witness God's ribbon cutting ceremony, and He wanted to make sure Joshua knew the battle belonged to the Lord before it even began.

Just because you're standing on the battleground doesn't mean it's your battle. Just because you'll see a victory doesn't mean it's your victory. To acknowledge God's holy ground in your life is to submit every inch of the battlefield, its outcomes, and its rewards, to Him.

Holy ground makes holy feet

God could have demolished Jericho like He did to Sodom and Gomorrah back in Abraham's day. You know, with flaming sulfur balls hurled from the sky. He could have asked Michael Bay to direct it. But God is infinitely creative and powerful, so He doesn't have to refer to His playbook. He has the luxury to set a new stage every time He wants to show off. Joshua didn't know it at the time, but his feet would play an important role in God's impending victory. These feet, now invited to touch holy ground, would be the ones that would simply march around the city and feel the walls crumble.

God wants to bring about more victories in your life, and in the lives of those around you. In many of these victories, He intends to use your faithful steps. But any step you take is only effective if you have taken the time to meet with God on holy ground. *Holy ground makes holy feet. Holy feet take holy steps. Holy steps topple strongholds in the name of Jesus.*

A lesson from the leaves

You can tell a thunderstorm is coming by the way the wind turns tree leaves upside down. This happens for two reasons: First, while "prevailing winds" are the winds that blow in the same general direction throughout the year, a storm generates localized wind that blows in directions the leaves aren't used to. But this only makes a difference because of the second reason: the leaf stems absorb the increased humidity before a storm, which allows them to flex and twist.

When God moves, He moves in ways that go against our normal ways of living and thinking. He's like a storm that blows against the prevailing winds. But just like leaves on a tree, we can recognize the time before He moves. While they soften in the humidity, we can soften in our humility (the wordplay was too good to pass up, and I won't apologize for it).

That's what this slow, quiet time before God's big move is about. Don't ask "God, are you with me?" Don't ask the wind to move in your direction. Instead, humble yourself to be able to move with it, and prepare to walk with holy feet.

Chapter Nine

The Victory

There's an old Monty Python sketch called the Ministry of Silly Walks. The premise is you can go to the Ministry of Silly Walks and apply for a government grant to help make your walk sillier. The Minister, of course, has the silliest walk of all, and he's walking around the office like a constipated giraffe with a stone in its shoe.

Throughout this book, we've talked about God's pace—often slower than we'd like—on the way to a goal. And we've said that if you're too focused on where you want to be, the goal, then you're missing the actual goal, which is the process of growing our hearts to be like the heart of Jesus. The growth is the goal. The process is the walk. We sometimes call our Christian life our "walk" with Jesus. That walk is going to look different—"silly", even.

Here are just some of the "silly" things we've had to do in our personal slow season: Trust in a God we can't see. Read, teach, and obey a book that is thousands of years old. Forgive people who haven't even apologized. Pray for healing. Wait for God to open doors instead of trying to force them open ourselves. Ask God to provide for specific needs like rent and new tires. Give more when we're earning less.

Reject some "good" opportunities because they don't line up with where we believe God is going.

The things God asks His people to do have never made sense to the rest of the world. Other people are going to think it looks foolish. Honestly, there are many times where you think your own walk is silly. But that just means you're trusting God even when it doesn't make sense.

This entire process of Joshua and Israel approaching the Promised Land doesn't make sense. Let's review the insanity for a moment, shall we?

Step one: make an alliance with a prostitute.

Step two: take a bath, literally and spiritually.

Step three: walk into a flood-stage river.

Step four: make two piles of rocks.

Step five: completely incapacitate every male for a few days.

Step six: celebrate a cultural feast in the enemy's territory.

Step seven: take off your sandals outside a paranoid, fortified city.

This isn't how armies conquer land. Sun Tzu didn't include these steps in *Art of War*. Where God leads, and more importantly, the way He leads us, may not make much sense. It may be unfamiliar or uncomfortable. It looks like a silly walk. Should we be surprised that God's plan to conquer the first city seems equally unreasonable? If you're familiar with the story of Joshua, pretend you're hearing this for the first time as you read what God told Joshua to tell the people:

> You and your fighting men should march around the
> town once a day for six days. Seven priests will walk
> ahead of the Ark, each carrying a ram's horn. On the

> seventh day you are to march around the town seven
> times, with the priests blowing the horns. When you
> hear the priests give one long blast on the rams' horns,
> have all the people shout as loud as they can. Then
> the walls of the town will collapse, and the people can
> charge straight into the town. (Joshua 6:3-5)

This is weird, right? Can we just admit it? It didn't make sense to the people in Jericho watching as each day, these foreign desert-wanderers walked around, silently, then went home. It didn't make sense to the Israelites, who probably felt like they were in the world's worst homecoming parade. This strategy (if you could call it that) required Israel to trust their leader. And this required Joshua to trust God.

"Trust in the Lord with all your heart; do not depend on your own understanding. Seek his will in all you do, and he will show you which path to take" (Proverbs 3:5-6).

It's easy to skim over the Bible verses in a book like this. Let's read it again, slower this time: "Trust in the Lord with all your heart; do not depend on your own understanding. Seek his will in all you do, and he will show you which path to take."

Don't depend on your own understanding. This is hard to obey. It's especially hard if you have a knack for gaining knowledge and understanding. After all, God gave us a brain; we have a responsibility to use it, right? Well, sure, but I think a major distinction can be made with the word that is translated "depend on" here, or "lean on" in other translations. It means to rest on, or rely on for support. More than He cares about you using your brain, God cares about what you rely on for support. And frankly, the only way to determine what you rely on for support is to bring you to a desperate position where you need support.

Fast forward with us in Israel's history. Long after Jericho. Israel was in the middle of a civil war. The Northern Kingdom was under the command of King Baasha. The Southern Kingdom (called Judah) was led by King Asa. Baasha was applying intense pressure on King Asa's smaller kingdom. Asa's entire territory was under siege, and he was running out of options.

Asa went to the temple of the Lord, but not to pray. Instead, he emptied the treasuries of God's temple and sent the stockpiles of silver and gold up to King Ben-hadad of the Arameans, along with a request that Ben-hadad break his treaty with Baasha. The Aramean king's loyalty could indeed be bought, so Ben-hadad accepted the bribe and proceeded to attack several of Baasha's towns until Baasha had to abandon the siege of Judah.

Asa relied on his own understanding. He assessed his options, made a decision, utilized his resources, and guess what? It worked! Well, by outward appearances, anyway...

At that time Hanani the seer came to King Asa and told him, "Because you have put your trust in the king of Aram instead of in the Lord your God, you missed your chance to destroy the army of the king of Aram. Don't you remember what happened to the Ethiopians and Libyans and their vast army, with all of their chariots and charioteers? At that time you relied on the Lord, and he handed them over to you. *The eyes of the Lord search the whole earth in order to strengthen those whose hearts are fully committed to him.* What a fool you have been! From now on you will be at war." (2 Chronicles 16:7-9, emphasis mine)

Your knowledge, wisdom, and understanding are like treasures that have been collected in the Lord's temple. They might give you access to opportunities and new options, but be careful to not rely on God's *presents* more than his *presence*. Otherwise, you, like King Asa, will "miss your chance" to see God bring about a total victory, and you may find yourself stuck fighting battles you were never intended to fight.

God is on a manhunt—not to destroy, but to strengthen. He's scouring the earth for people who trust in Him with all their heart. He knows how draining that can be. That's why He promises to strengthen those fully committed hearts.

Your own understanding is weak and incomplete. It cannot be leaned on without eventually breaking. God doesn't promise to strengthen your understanding. He promises to strengthen your heart when you choose to trust Him beyond what you can understand.

This verse is so integral to walking with the Lord, and worth memorizing, so let's visit it again: "Trust in the Lord with all your heart; do not depend on your own understanding. Seek his will in all you do, and he will show you which path to take" (Proverbs 3:5-6).

Your path may take you around and around and around the goal. Maybe the goal is something you've wanted for a long time. Maybe it's an obstacle or difficulty you've wished would go away for a long time. You either want to get there, or you want to get it behind you. But God's path doesn't make any sense.

If you trust in the Lord with all your heart, and you don't depend on your own understanding of the situation, *and* if you seek God's will in all you do... then He'll show you which path to take. And when you see that path, or when you are on that path, don't be surprised if it seems weird.

Weird wins

Joshua's path around the city looked foolish to other warriors. Peter's path across the water looked reckless to the other disciples. Jesus' path to the cross looked like defeat to everyone but His Father. God's path for you, if you are willing to stay on it, looks just as unlikely.

You're going to be tempted to stop. "Why do I keep praying? Why did I give that money? Why did I give up that job or promotion? Why did we move states?" Don't stop. Keep going down that weird path God put you on. In fact, be excited you're on it! Why? Because *a weird walk leads to weird wins.*

"When the people heard the sound of the rams' horns, they shouted as loud as they could. Suddenly, the walls of Jericho collapsed, and the Israelites charged straight into the town and captured it" (Joshua 6:20).

God seems to enjoy weird wins. All throughout the Old Testament, we see God giving strange instructions to His people. Noah, build a boat in the wilderness. Abraham, pack up and leave to go somewhere else. Israel, look at this bronze snake to be healed. It only makes sense after the fact.

Nobody would willingly write this stuff. Honestly, it's one of the reasons why I believe the Bible is true, because this isn't what humans would come up with or keep around for thousands of years. The Bible doesn't make humans look good. It doesn't make religious leaders look good. It doesn't make political leaders look good. It doesn't encourage us to do what feels right to us, but instead it appeals to some authority outside ourselves. It only makes God look good, despite our best and worst efforts. It's a weird book, and living by it makes for a weird life.

If you want God's win, be ready to do something weird.

You may still be stuck on the word "weird".

We were at our friends' house one evening, and their pre-teen son showed Kelsey one of his crazy creations in a video game. "Hah! That's great. You're so weird!"

He recoiled and genuinely tried to defend himself, "I'm not weird!"

Recognizing she may have unintentionally done some harm, she explained to him that in our family, we use the word "weird" as a compliment. It means thinking outside the box, being creative, and being bold enough to let others see it.

This culture has made it so that "weird" is a bad word. Most people don't want to be weird. Most people want to be average. Average is safe. Blend in. But God didn't bring His

IF YOU WANT GOD'S WIN, BE READY TO DO SOMETHING WEIRD.

people all the way to the Promised Land so they could blend in! The entire process wasn't to transform them into looking like everybody else.

God still asks strange things of His people today. He asks us to give generously. The world thinks that's weird. He asks us to love and forgive those who hate us. That's not natural. That's weird. People don't get it. They see us pray, they see us go to church, they see us read our Bibles, and it looks to them like we're just walking around in circles.

Seriously! We're supposed to live according to a book that was written thousands of years ago, and pray to a God nobody can see, in the name of Jesus who, somehow, is both God but also came as a baby, and died, but also came back to life—none of this makes any sense!

"Oh no, Mike's having an existential crisis."

No—well, maybe, but hear me out—God's plan for victory, not just here at Jericho, but His entire grand plan for humanity, doesn't make any sense. The apostle Paul says it himself:

The message of the cross is foolish to those who are headed for destruction! But we who are being saved know it is the very power of God. As the Scriptures say, "I will destroy the wisdom of the wise and discard the intelligence of the intelligent."

So where does this leave the philosophers, the scholars, and the world's brilliant debaters? God has made the wisdom of this world look foolish. Since God in his wisdom saw to it that the world would never know him through human wisdom, he has used our foolish preaching to save those who believe. It is foolish to the Jews, who ask for signs from heaven. And it is foolish to the Greeks, who seek human wisdom. So when we preach that Christ was crucified, the Jews are offended and the Gentiles say it's all nonsense.

"But to those called by God to salvation, both Jews and Gentiles, Christ is the power of God and the wisdom of God. This foolish plan of God is wiser than the wisest of human plans, and God's weakness is stronger than the greatest of human strength" (1 Corinthians 1:18-25).

There are some amazing, bold statements in there. Christ is the power of God and the wisdom of God. Following Christ is going to make you feel weak and foolish, because it's based on God's power and wisdom, not yours. And since your own strength and understanding aren't enough to get you where you need to be, that's why God calls you to have faith.

Disproportionate results

There is nothing about a week's worth of walking around Jericho that should have made it fall. Even the seventh day's seven-revolution trip with its loud trumpet blasts shouldn't have had a physical impact on Jericho. Yet, that was exactly the formula God decreed for this particular victory.

It doesn't add up. The dots don't connect. When was the last time you felt that way about your circumstances? When we throw our hands up in the air and say, "I have no idea! It's impossible!", that's where God likes to operate. Jesus was constantly leading his disciples up to—and off—the edge of what makes sense.

Thousands of listeners needed a meal. "You feed them!"

We need to pay the temple tax. "Catch a fish and look in its mouth!"

We've been fishing all night and haven't caught a thing. "Throw your net on the other side of a boat!"

It required faith to take a step beyond reason in these situations. And each time, there was a disproportionately large outcome. Every listener was full, with leftovers. A coin for the exact needed amount was found inside the first fish caught. One hundred and fifty-three fish filled a net that could barely be towed to shore. Faith results in disproportionate impact.

Now is a good time to warn, however, that there are too many teachers who talk about faith like it's some unseen force that gives you superpowers, if you know how to tap into it. Faith isn't a force to leverage. "Faith is confidence in what we hope for and assurance about what we do not see" (Hebrews 11:1, NIV). *Faith doesn't force God's hand; it reaches for God's hand.* It says, "I don't need to see a way through this. I need you." And God is eager to show you that your faith is well-placed. Then, when God pulls off a victory only He could have done, you know where the credit has to be given.

Taking credit

In the days when Paul was writing letters to churches across the Mediterranean coast, the Roman Empire would have parades—called triumphs—celebrating victories over their enemies. The main feature of the parade would be the victorious general or emperor riding in a chariot, followed by the spoils of war: artifacts, goods, and a procession of chained captives. Attendees of these *triumphs* would wave flowers, burn incense, and sprinkle perfume to fill the air with the aroma of victory. The fame of the victorious leader would spread, increasing awe in the view of those in favor of the leader, and dread in the eyes of those opposed.

When Paul wrote to the church in Corinth, he used a metaphor that would have resonated with his first-century audience:

> But thank God! He has made us his captives and continues to lead us along in Christ's triumphal procession. Now he uses us to spread the knowledge of Christ everywhere, like a sweet perfume. Our lives are a Christ-like fragrance rising up to God. But this fragrance is perceived differently by those who are being saved and by those who are perishing. To those who are perishing, we are a dreadful smell of death and doom. But to those who are being saved, we are a life-giving perfume. (2 Corinthians 2:14-16)

This is why Jesus wants to win victories in your life. It's not to give you a comfortable life. He loves you, but Jesus is not your flight attendant; your safety and comfort are not his priorities for the duration of the flight. Instead, Jesus wants to show off like a victorious king. You are one of His prized trophies. He gets to point at you, the changes He's made in your life, and the impossible things He's done in and through you, and say, "Look, everyone! People said it couldn't be done, but I did it! Darkness tried to stop me, but I can't be stopped! Sin and death have to bow to me!"

The aroma of what God has done in your life is meant to fill the air around you. To those who resist and avoid Jesus, you smell like death. It's nothing personal; God's victories in your life spell out death to their plans and rebellion. But to those who recognize their need for a savior and want to see a victory in their own lives, you smell like life and hope.

The rest of the world is looking to be the champions of their own stories. They get knocked down, but they get up again. They go from rags to riches. They pick themselves up by the bootstraps. They do it their way. And you know what? Quite a few of them do achieve their goals. Many of the most successful people today (by the world's standards) were underdogs who dug deep to accomplish what others said couldn't be done. Good for them. But their win is an explainable win. They can point to their efforts, being in the right place at the right time, and their go-getter attitude. As a result, they can get the credit for the win.

God isn't interested in explainable wins. He wants to win victories that have no explanation other than, "God did it." If God is going to win such victories in your life, you will have to give up the strengths you typically rely on.

In Jeremiah 9:23-24, we read the words of God, "Don't let the wise boast in their wisdom, or the powerful boast in their power, or the rich boast in their riches. But those who wish to boast should boast in this alone: that they truly know me and understand that I am the Lord who demonstrates unfailing love and who brings justice and righteousness to the earth, and that I delight in these things."

Living a life of weird wins means you only get to boast in the fact that you get to know God more and more as you become less and less. You don't get credit for God's weird wins. But you *do* receive a deeper knowledge of God, and a better understanding of how He works. You see His unfailing love, justice and righteousness. He loves this stuff. And He wants to work these weird wins throughout your life.

Chapter Ten

The Conviction

When I (Mike) was about eight years old, our church had a room filled with craft supplies, paper, Flannelgraphs (church kids of the 80s and 90s know), and all sorts of props. At the time, one of my mother's church roles was "Resource Room Coordinator," and she was in charge of organizing, stocking, and keeping inventory of this room.

You might not know this about me, but I was a pretty big deal back then. Not only was my mom the Resource Room Coordinator, but she also taught my Sunday School class. So, yeah, these were my stomping grounds.

One day, as I was watching my mom unpack a new box of supplies, she pulled out a large bag of gold coins. My eight-year-old brain may have exaggerated their beauty and value, but I was enthralled with them. "Ooh can I have one?"

"No, these are for thuhbermbashurble..." I don't actually remember what she said they were for. I stopped listening after "no."

That weekend at church, while my mom was busy doing some boring grown-up thing, I went upstairs to the Resource Room. I just wanted to look at the pretty coins again. I turned on the light—wait, no, turn them off again—better not draw attention in case some-one walks by. I squinted around the room, and spied the bag of coins. So pretty! Who was I kidding; I didn't just want to *look* at the coins. I wanted to take one. Just one, though! The bag contained, what—quick eight-year-old math—ten thousand? Nobody would even know one was missing! I just need to unzip the bag, slip my tiny fingers inside and—oh, shoot. It's not a zip-top bag; it's sealed shut. Hmm... no problem. I'll just poke a little hole in the corner of the bag, spread it out to be just big enough for one coin, and... got it!

After repositioning the bag so the hole was not facing out, I emerged from the dark room with my new prize. It really was as beautiful as I hoped it would be! I admired it all the way down the stairs and into the Fellowship Hall. I was dexterously flipping it over my fingers, and flicking it up into the air and catching it like a newsie who earned his first silver dollar.

Then, inexplicably, I fumbled the coin, and snatched at the air as it fell to the ground. But it did not do me the favor of falling flat at my feet to be easily reclaimed. No, it landed on its edge and rolled. It rolled across the hardwood floor, seeming to accelerate the more I chased it. It swerved left and right, dodging adult shoes and floorboard cracks—how was the room this long?—until my outstretched arm was just about within reach. Just when I was about to make my final, victorious lunge, the coin disappeared—SNAP!—under the toe of a woefully familiar high heel shoe. My eyes scanned upward cautiously, but were not surprised to find my cross-armed mother glaring down at me disapprovingly.

As the walls of Jericho were on their way down, Joshua commanded all the people, "Jericho and everything in it must be completely destroyed as an offering to the Lord. Only Rahab the prostitute and the others in her house will be spared, for she protected our spies. Do not take any of the things set apart for destruction, or you yourselves will be completely destroyed, and you will bring trouble on the camp of Israel. Everything made from silver, gold, bronze, or iron is sacred to the Lord and must be brought into his treasury" (Joshua 6:17-19).

Everything? Like an eight-year old boy eyeing a big see-through bag of plastic gold coins, the Israelites could have thought, "But... I'm sure it won't matter if a little bit comes home with me, right?" Surely, each silver spoon or gold candlestick would make for a nice, little nest-egg as they started to settle into their new home. Every bronze shield and iron sword would come in handy in the upcoming battles.

And why would God want it in His treasury anyway? He doesn't need it. He's God. He doesn't need this sword. I do. What would He even do with some silver coins? And look at that luxurious Babylonian robe! Burn it? What a waste!

But, hey—God brought the walls down; He can call the shots. If He wants to keep the loot for Himself, I guess He earned it, right?

Eventually, Jericho's dust settled, and smoke rose. The men sorted everything they could find. If it could burn, they burned it. If it couldn't, it was brought to the priests in charge of God's treasury. Joshua, riding the high of God's overwhelming victory, set his sights on the next town over: Ai. The scouting report suggested only a small group of fighters was necessary. No need to send everybody.

The small army marched in the confidence that God would defeat each city of the Promised Land. If He did what He did in Jericho, imagine the cake walk Ai would be!

It was not a cake walk. It was a pie in the face. Israel lost thirty-six men as they were soundly routed by a handful of locals. The shocked

Israelites were stunned and lost all the courage they had built up from Jericho.

The real momentum killer

When was the last time you felt like you were "in a groove"? Confidence was high, momentum was picking up, everything seemed to be going your way. Maybe you're there now. That's great. How about a time when things seemed to flip? Things that used to come easy to you, all of a sudden felt like a struggle. Relationships turned sour. Confidence plummeted. Maybe you're there now. It doesn't feel so great. You can't help but ask, "Why did this happen? What's going on?"

Frankly, there could be any number of explanations, but that's part of the frustration. Joshua fell to his face and cried out to God, "Oh, Sovereign Lord, why did you bring us across the Jordan River if you are going to let the Amorites kill us? If only we had been content to stay on the other side! Lord, what can I say now that Israel has fled from its enemies? For when the Canaanites and all the other people living in the land hear about it, they will surround us and wipe our name off the face of the earth. And then what will happen to the honor of your great name?" (Joshua 7:7-9)

I love Joshua's heartbroken response. He was convinced it wasn't God's fault; it had to be his own sinful heart. Is it because we weren't content with what you had given us? If so, I'm sorry, but now we'll be a laughingstock among our neighbors, and you'll lose your reputation here!

God told Joshua to get up off his face. The reason was simple: "Israel has sinned and broken my covenant! They have stolen some of the things that I commanded must be set apart for me. And they have not only stolen them but have lied about it and hidden the things among their own belongings" (Joshua 7:11).

Pulling this thing over

My (Kelsey's) grandfather was a kind and gentle man. When Grandpa raised his voice, the family listened. My mom recalls long road trips during which she and her siblings were arguing while Grandpa was driving. He would announce sternly from behind the wheel, "Stop that or else I will pull this car over!" And the squabble stopped. Later, as young adults, my mom and her sister asked him, "Out of curiosity, what would you have done if we didn't stop, and you pulled the car over?"

He chuckled, "Honestly, I don't know. I was just hoping it wouldn't get to that point!"

Well, Israel got to that point. And God did know what He would do. God warned them at Jericho that disobedience would result in trouble. Now there was trouble. Like we've said, God cares more about the process than the victory. As long as there was still disobedience among God's people, victory would not be an option. So God pulled the car over. And unlike Kelsey's grandfather, God knew what He was going to do about it.

"Command the people to purify themselves in preparation for tomorrow. For this is what the Lord, the God of Israel, says: Hidden among you, O Israel, are things set apart for the Lord. You will never defeat your enemies until you remove these things from among you" (Joshua 7:13).

Tomorrow? God could have struck the guilty party with lightning and been done with it. But we shouldn't be surprised to recognize that God is willing to wait out the process instead of jumping right to the end of the matter. Can you imagine the tension in the Israelite camp that night? The whispers, the accusations, the lack of sleep? This time of tension was, in fact, a provision of God's patience. Would the guilty party come forward willingly? Would they allow the upheaval of their conscience to do its job and motivate them to make things right?

Time to come forward

The next day, God first called out the tribe of the guilty party. Judah.

Judah? The lion? The tribe that will hold the scepter? No way! Everyone's eyes widened. Eleven other tribes relaxed. Judahites stepped forward, wide-eyed in fear.

Then the clan. Zerah. The rest of the clans of Judah breathed a sigh of relief.

Then the family. Zimri's family. Zimri's wife clutched his arm in fear. He shook his head in disbelief. Zimri and his sons, daughters, and grandchildren stepped forward reluctantly.

Then, one by one, the family members were presented to God. Is it him? No. Is it her? No. All the way down the line. Tension mounted. Is it him? ... Yes.

Achan.

Joshua was devastated and pleaded with Achan. "My son, give glory to the Lord, the God of Israel, by telling the truth. Make your confession and tell me what you have done. Don't hide it from me."

"Achan replied, 'It is true! I have sinned against the Lord, the God of Israel. Among the plunder I saw a beautiful robe from Babylon, 200 silver coins, and a bar of gold weighing more than a pound. I wanted them so much that I took them. They are hidden in the ground beneath my tent, with the silver buried deeper than the rest'" (Joshua 7:19-21).

Achan had been aware of what he was doing. He dug a hole in his tent so he could cover up his sin in private. In fact, he dug two layers of a hole, so just in case the top layer was confiscated, he could keep the deeper silver. This wasn't a matter of "Oh! I didn't hear the command!" Achan knew God's warning about Jericho. He understood God's plunder was off limits.

So why did he keep it?

Well, why did Kelsey and I keep it?

The hole in our tent

When we got engaged, we were 21 and 22 years old. We were both blessed with parents who didn't put their burdens on their kids, we had never knowingly faced financial hardship. Sure, our parents had struggled at times, but as kids, we thought everything was great all the time. We were never rich by our own perspective, but we had clothes on our backs, college tuition paid for, vehicles gifted to us, and our whole lives ahead of us.

It was in this state of life that we declared a value for our new family, "We will always tithe. No matter what."

And we did. The first decade of married life, through better or worse, richer or poorer, we always gave back to God at least 10% of our income. Income was irregular in gig-based ministry, but we always tithed. Rent was always covered. Bills were always paid on time. Rent was always ready on the first of the month.

Until 2020. Elsewhere, we've mentioned the financial impact on our family when the quarantine shut down the Christian event industry. Financially, we had never been worse off. Everything went on a credit card, and we never had enough to pay it off at the end of the month. With the negative balance building, we stopped tithing.

We never had a lot. But when "a little" turned into "nothing," it was really hard to believe God still wanted us to tithe. He didn't need it; we did. We needed every dollar. We genuinely thought that keeping $100 would make a bigger difference in our situation than being obedient would. Obedience doesn't pay the bills. Dollars do.

Or so we thought.

Disobedience resulted in more debt than we had seen in our lives. We can't change the past or know an alternate reality, but we firmly believe that if we had tithed, we would not have incurred the debt we did. How are we so certain? Because every other season of our marriage when we *did* commit to a tithe, no matter how little we were making, we did not go into debt. Things simply worked out, sometimes without explanation.

What about you? Why might you hold on to something God has told you to give up? Why might you keep when He says "let go"? Hold on when He says "give"? In our minds, we stopped tithing when we felt like God didn't need our money as much as we needed it. It ultimately came down to a distortion of what we valued: *we valued money and the security we thought it provided more than we valued obeying God.*

I think Achan was sick of being a wandering vagabond. He was tired of waiting for God to deliver on this "land flowing with milk and honey" idea his grandparents talked about. God had brought them to a land of prosperity and Achan had the idea that some of it could be his. God didn't need it as much as he did. He genuinely thought keeping a few items buried under his tent would make a bigger difference in his life than being obedient would.

God gave Achan time to confess. Even as God was zeroing in on the culprit, there were several opportunities for Achan to step forward willingly. By the time he was in the hotseat, it was too late. He and his family bore the fatal consequences of his sin. Who knows what mercy God may have been willing to show if he confessed earlier?

I don't remember what punishment resulted from my Sunday School crime. Whatever it was, it was enough. I learned the hard way that God collaborated with my parents when it came to exposing my sin. To this day, I credit God for popping that coin out of my hand and guiding its roll directly to my mother at the end of the room. But I learned another lesson the following Sunday.

Sunday School was coming to a close for the day. My mother, as she has always enjoyed doing, pulled out some props to help us remember the story. Among them was a bag of beautiful gold coins. She took a handful and started handing one to each student. They eagerly held out their hands, joyfully received their token, and my heart sank in shame. I didn't even hold out my hand. But my mother didn't skip over me. It would have been fair if she had. Instead, she took my hand and placed a coin in it, a somber reminder that God is willing to provide, but I must submit to His timing and His way.

The sad thing is, if Achan had waited for God's timing for provision, he would have enjoyed the plunder of the very next city God handed to Israel in battle.

"Do not be afraid or discouraged. Take all your fighting men and attack Ai, for I have given you the king of Ai, his people, his town, and his land. You will destroy them as you destroyed Jericho and its king. *But this time you may keep the plunder and the livestock for yourselves.*" (Joshua 8:1-2, emphasis mine)

This time. I shudder to think about how much I've missed out on *this time*, because I was starving to grab what I wanted *last time*. When the walls finally fall, goal-thinking will spur you to rush in and take what you've been so desperately waiting for. But when growth is the goal, obedience always has to come first.

God is especially mindful of the things we want more than we want Him. Sometimes, He lets people get the things they want, to discover the hard way that they can't replace God. Other times, He denies their desires and works with them to change their desires over time to be aligned with His. God's slowness is grace. He may be moving slower than you want Him to, but His goal is to keep you and your heart close to Him, for your good.

Chapter Eleven

The Commitment

If you continue reading the book of Joshua, and I hope you do, you'll find that God worked weird wins throughout the book. They weren't all victories in the typical sense. But God used every battle, every win, every loss, and every unlikely tactic to help transform them into who they needed to be—God's people in His Promised Land.

Before we call it a day and go our separate ways, let's skip ahead to the end of the book of Joshua, where we find Joshua and the people of Israel gathered together in one place. They, too, are ready to go their separate ways. They've conquered vast regions and divided the land among all the tribes. But before they disperse to live their new lives, Joshua gives a final exhortation in a town called Shechem. Not coincidentally, Shechem was where God appeared to Abraham to promise this land to his nation of descendants. Inspired by this significant location in the history of God's people, Joshua recaps their entire history, starting with Abraham, Isaac, Jacob, Joseph in Egypt, slavery, Moses leading them out, and all of God's weird wins up to this point.

He continues, speaking on behalf of the Lord, "It was not your swords or bows that brought you victory. I gave you land you had not worked on, and I gave you towns you did not build—the towns where you are now living. I gave you vineyards and olive groves for food, though you did not plant them" (Joshua 24:12-13).

Allow the Word of God to speak to you directly for a few moments. Hear God pointing to various aspects of your life, "You didn't earn any of this! I promised to take care of you, and I single-handedly kept my promise, and then some! You didn't earn any good thing you have in your life. Your job, your money, your family, your home—you only have it because I gave it to you."

What does Joshua say to do in response?

"So fear the Lord and serve him wholeheartedly. Put away forever the idols your ancestors worshiped when they lived beyond the Euphrates River and in Egypt. Serve the Lord alone. But if you refuse to serve the Lord, then choose today whom you will serve. Would you prefer the gods your ancestors served beyond the Euphrates? Or will it be the gods of the Amorites in whose land you now live?" (Joshua 24:14-15).

Talk of gods and idols tends to switch *off* the part of our brain that alerts us, "Hey, this affects you, so pay attention!" Idols and gods feel like ancient biblical things that people were involved in before advanced economy, government, and medicine. But if you consider why those people interacted with gods and idols, I believe you'll find idolatry is alive and well today—even, perhaps, in your own life.

What works?

The prophet Jeremiah spent his entire ministry attempting to convince Israel that God's patience surrounding their idolatry was going to come to an end if they didn't repent. They would be removed from their beloved Promised Land.

Check out this fascinating response from actual Israelites steeped in worshiping an Egyptian god:

> We will not listen to your messages from the Lord! We will do whatever we want. We will burn incense and pour out liquid offerings to the Queen of Heaven just as much as we like—just as we, and our ancestors, and our kings and officials have always done in the towns of Judah and in the streets of Jerusalem. For in those days we had plenty to eat, and we were well off and had no troubles! But ever since we quit burning incense to the Queen of Heaven and stopped worshiping her with liquid offerings, we have been in great trouble and have been dying from war and famine. (Jeremiah 44:16-18)

The Israelites found a connection between worshiping some god (a demon, really, as Moses calls out in Deuteronomy 32:16-17) and receiving what they want—a sense of provision and protection. We learn from Jesus' episode of being tempted by Satan in Matthew 4 that demons want to be worshipped, and have some level of authority to reward those who worship them. Why else would these ancient people go to such extreme measures to worship these demons, including cutting themselves and sacrificing their children, if they didn't benefit from it in some way?

When you boil it down, *we worship what works.* Satan is willing and able to give you what works temporarily in order to keep you from finding what works for eternity. God continually demonstrates that He is the God above all gods (Psalm 95:3), and He alone can provide lasting peace, hope, and love. If there is a "catch" with God's proposal, however, it's this: you can't just get what you need from God and go about your life. God's way requires surrendering to His will as He completely renovates your very being. That feels like too steep a price to pay for those who don't like having to answer to anyone else. So Satan is quick to offer another deal.

WE WORSHIP WHAT WORKS.

You may not have physical idols around your house, but you have something that "works." You have something you go to when you need something. You swipe that card, you transfer that money, you drink that drink, you put on that attitude. *Your first call, your first resort, your first reaction to deal with a situation—that's your idol.*

You might idolize *worry*. "I don't want to worry, I just can't help it." I didn't say you want to do it, but when your first reaction is thinking about what could go wrong, and telling yourself negative stories that haven't happened yet... instead of bringing your concerns to God? You just sacrificed to the idol of worry. You sacrificed your peace.

You might idolize *gossip*. Someone offends you, and instead of taking it to God, asking Him to give you strength and wisdom to approach the other person, you go to get other people's opinions. Or you're not the offended party at all, but you became aware of something that will serve as a good conversation starter with someone else.

Gossip is a fake connection built on brokenness. You just sacrificed to the idol of gossip. You sacrificed unity.

You might idolize your *reputation*. You feel like God is asking you to do something, but it's going to look weird to people. Instead of going to God first and asking, "God, how do you see me? Who do you say I am?", you ask yourself, "How will other people see me? How does this affect me?" You just sacrificed to the idol of your own reputation. You sacrificed humility.

You might idolize *religion*. You come to church, even on Wednesday nights, because you're hoping to impress God. You give money, you pray twice a day, you sing the songs. But it's all to make yourself feel better, like you're doing the right thing. You make sacrifices to the idol of religion. You sacrifice a relationship with God.

Remember earlier, when we talked about God clarifying for Joshua that He is not picking sides. God is not on your side. He's asking you "are you on my side? Are you with me?" Similarly, Joshua draws a line in the sand and says, "Look, I know what your family has a habit of relying on. I know the people around you have their ways of doing things. I know you will not be popular in the culture around you. But you need to make a choice for yourself. Are you with God?"

If you refuse to serve the Lord, then choose today whom you will serve. Worry? Gossip? Your reputation? Your bank account? Choose today—today!—don't leave it up to chance or feelings later. Choose today who you will serve.

Joshua led by example, "But as for me and my family, we will serve the Lord" (Joshua 24:15).

It's a bold, beautiful statement. We see this on Hobby Lobby art; church goers from the 90s can probably hum the tune for the lyric, "As for me and my house, we will serve the Lord!" It's a nice verse. But remember who Joshua is talking to; he's not talking to unbelievers. He's talking to God's people!

And no doubt, they're reacting like you're reacting right now. "Yeah! Totally! We get it! We serve the Lord!" Look at their reaction:

"The people replied, 'We would never abandon the Lord and serve other gods. For the Lord our God is the one who rescued us and our ancestors from slavery in the land of Egypt. He performed mighty miracles before our very eyes. As we traveled through the wilderness among our enemies, he preserved us. It was the Lord who drove out the Amorites and the other nations living here in the land. So we, too, will serve the Lord, for he alone is our God'" (Joshua 24:16-18).

Right? They're thinking, "Joshua, I get it!" And again, you're thinking, "Mike, I get it! I'm convinced! I'm reading this book about Joshua! I bought twelve copies and handed them out to my friends and family! Of course I'll serve the Lord!"

Well, thank you; that's very generous of you. And if it were me, I'd shake your hand and wish you well. But Joshua doesn't let his people off the hook so easily.

"You are not able to serve the Lord, for he is a holy and jealous God. He will not forgive your rebellion and your sins. If you abandon the Lord and serve other gods, he will turn against you and destroy you, even though he has been so good to you" (Joshua 24:19-20).

"You're not able to serve the Lord?" Who does this guy think he is? And before we get too offended on Israel's behalf, let's again let the Word of God do what it does and speak to our hearts, and ask ourselves: Who are we to think that we can serve the Lord Almighty, Creator of Heaven and Earth? What, because we come to church? Maybe serve on a team? Because we felt generous once and dropped a twenty in the bucket? Because we pray before falling asleep? We say we want to spend eternity with Him, but are we willing to spend an hour with Him today? We ask Him to use us, but are our hands full, trying to hold on to our own time, resources, understanding, and reputation?

Joshua highlights two highly misunderstood qualities of God: God is holy and jealous. Holy, which means that He won't tolerate a single sin, and jealous, that it breaks His heart to see you prefer your little sin over Him. Choose today whom you will serve.

You may still be like, "Right! I know!" Okay, let's wrap this up:

"But the people answered Joshua, "No, we will serve the Lord!"

"You are a witness to your own decision," Joshua said. "You have chosen to serve the Lord."

"Yes," they replied, "we are witnesses to what we have said."

"All right then," Joshua said, "destroy the idols among you, and turn your hearts to the Lord, the God of Israel."

The people said to Joshua, "We will serve the Lord our God. We will obey him alone."

So Joshua made a covenant with the people that day at Shechem, committing them to follow the decrees and regulations of the Lord. Joshua recorded these things in the Book of God's Instructions. As a reminder of their agreement, he took a huge stone and rolled it beneath the terebinth tree beside the Tabernacle of the Lord.

Joshua said to all the people, "This stone has heard everything the Lord said to us. It will be a witness to testify against you if you go back on your word to God." Then Joshua sent all the people away to their own homelands. (Joshua 24:21-28)

Joshua made another memorial. So, before I send you away to your homeland... we're going to make another memorial.

In just a minute, you'll find a blank line, and I'd encourage you to physically sign it. But of course, you'd like to know what exactly you're signing. For that, let me fast forward to Micah chapter 6, where we realize God's people, in fact, did not keep their commitment at Shechem. They slowly drifted back into obscene idolatry, while continuing to claim the title of "God's people." God, through the prophet Micah, invited His people to think back and walk with Him again:

"And remember your journey from Acacia Grove to Gilgal, when I, the Lord, did everything I could to teach you about my faithfulness" (Micah 6:5).

Acacia Grove to Gilgal. That covers everything we talked about in this book. That's everything from sending out the spies to launching an attack on Jericho. Can you believe the actual "length" of this journey from Acacia Grove to Gilgal is only about 8 miles? It probably took you longer to read this book than it would take to walk between the two. And yet, the Israelite's journey to Jericho—and your journey to and through the impossible obstacles in your life—is fraught with epic waits, pains, and lessons learned the hard way. Why? Because all the while, God has been doing everything He can to teach you about His faithfulness.

The only thing He asks in return is your faithfulness.

Does faithfulness have to look like great sacrifices of time and energy and resources? Micah goes on to explain, "No, O people, the Lord has told you what is good, and this is what he requires of you: to do what is right, to love mercy, and to walk humbly with your God" (Micah 6:8).

Let this be our stone rolled under the terebinth tree in Shechem, a commitment to honor God's faithfulness with our own. And because none of us should go about this alone, Kelsey and I have signed this commitment, and we invite you to join us:

Thank you, Lord, for demonstrating your faithfulness from the River to the Fortress, and for helping my heart grow to be more like yours along the way.

I commit to this continued work until it's complete in the ultimate Promised Land, eternity with You.

I commit to do what is right, as described in Your Word, to love mercy, as you have offered to me, and to walk humbly with You, my God, as demonstrated by Jesus.

Signed,

Michael Domeny
____

Kelsey Domeny
____

____

(this one's for you!)

Works Cited

[1] Swindoll, C. [@chuckswindoll]. (2026, January 3). *When I ask peo-ple when they really grew spiritually, they never describe an easy time. Never. [Post]. X. https://x.com/chuckswindoll/status/2007436807768 596630*

[2] NewSong. "Before the Day." *Rescue (Trax),* Integrity Music, 2005.

About the Authors

Mike and Kelsey have served in creative ministry together since 2009. This has taken various forms. Mike has traveled full-time with *321 Improv* and wrote a book, *Thrown off Script* based on his ex-  perience. Kelsey has directed, written, and produced programs and videos for churches across the country. At the core of their work, their desire is to empower Christians understand the Bible and do something about it.

Together, they formed **Outloud Bible** (outloudbible.com), where they produce podcasts, study material, and live performances of the Bible so people can hear it, love it, and live it.

They live in New Hampshire with their daughter, Addy, and their bunny, Cinnabun.

Encourage, **entertain**, and **equip**
your audience at your next
conference, retreat, or gathering.

How can we serve you and your event?

It's our goal to give you the peace of mind that
your speakers are low-maintenance,
audience-minded, veterans of the stage,
and to help your people understand the Bible
and do something about it.

to invite Mike and Kelsey to speak
at your event, inquire at **outloudbible**.com

HEAR IT. LOVE IT. LIVE IT.

UNFORGETTABLE, ENGAGING
BIBLE READINGS

Ignite hunger for the Word of God
with **powerful and easy-to-understand**
Bible readings for your church or event.

"very moving and **fun**"
- Michael M.

"remarkably **fresh**"
- Jerry J.

"Our church and community
came to see a performance.
They left with a **greater
understanding of Scripture**."
- Rob Willis, Journey Church

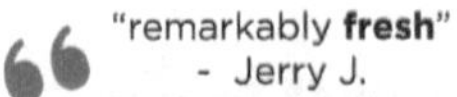

20-minute episodes
of engaging reading and application

Listen wherever you listen to podcasts

learn more at **outloudbible**.com

www.ingramcontent.com/pod-product-compliance
Lightning Source LLC
Chambersburg PA
CBHW030858120726
48008CB00002B/35